THE *Angel Lady*

THE *Angel Lady*

A Journey with My Spiritual Companions

Dear Eleanor & John, God be with You,

Susan Reynolds

authorHOUSE®

Susan Reynolds

AuthorHouse™
1663 Liberty Drive
Bloomington, IN 47403
www.authorhouse.com
Phone: 1-800-839-8640

Published by AuthorHouse   12/10/2012

ISBN: 978-1-4772-9565-6 (sc)
ISBN: 978-1-4772-9564-9 (hc)
ISBN: 978-1-4772-9563-2 (e)

Library of Congress Control Number: 2012922807

Contents

Preface

Consider this book an invitation to walk side-by-side with me as we journey through my life with my spiritual companions. This book was written with great trepidation. It leaves my life wide open to scrutiny and debate. However, as with many of you, sometimes you have to let go of the fear and free fall into the arms of The One Who Created You.

We all are concerned about what others think of us. Let's face it, who can honestly say they don't care what others think? However, this was written with all of you in mind. All of us who have struggled with pain, suffering, tragedy, and most of all great joy. This is a walk that has twists, turns, and a great sense of purpose. If you have ever experienced a sense of The Divine, an Angel, or the nearness of someone who has passed into the next life, this book is essentially about your story; your journey.

For me, this was my way of giving gratitude and honor to God for all of the blessings in my life. Perhaps you may feel the same about your life . . . grateful. So let's lock arms and experience this together.

Acknowledgements

- First and foremost I must give thanks to God for all that I am, all that I have, and all those who have blessed my life with their presence.

- To my husband Deacon Jerry, you have always been there for me and have showered me with compassion, encouragement and great love. I Love You. If it weren't for your persistence, this book would have never been written.

- To my son Michael, my daughter-in-law Kristina, and my beautiful grandchildren Anthony and Alyssa, you are my joy and pure gifts from God.

- To all of my family, especially those who are looking down from heaven and wondering why it took me so long to write this, you are always in my heart.

- To all those who contributed to this story, thank you for your love and support.

- To all the volunteers, guests and supporters who worked tirelessly, out of love for God and one another at The Follow Me Foundation, thank you.

- To those who have prayed, laughed and shared their lives with me, none of this would have been possible without you. You know who you are.

- To Francine Gillen who continues to inspire so many with her beautiful, sacred art.

- Last but certainly not least, to my sister in Christ, my editor, LaJoyce Brookshire, you are a light to this world.

Chapter One

Introduction to Life

Once upon a time is the usual way a fairy tale begins. This however is no fairy tale. I know this because I lived it. Reading these accounts may have you wondering, scratching your head if this really *is* some fairy tale made-up in my head. I can assure you; these events are real and true.

I was born in The Bronx, New York on November 12, 1957 to Susie and Benny Cusimano, and I am the third and youngest child of three. We were a typical Italian-Catholic family growing up with relatives, siblings and friends (seen and unseen), and always gathering for one event or another. My parents came from very large families, eight children on each side of the family, as well as eighteen children born of their grandparents . . . each. Whew!

My mother had a total of seven children, but only three of us survived. Mommy had a strong, lively faith. Daddy, a quiet, strong, and enduring faith. My maternal grandmother Rose, also known as Grandma, was what one might call very religious and mystical. As the story goes, my Uncle Frankie was accidentally shot by a friend as a teen, Grandma stayed at home to pray. Miraculously, as she prayed by the window, a dove appeared and she was instantly shown that two doctors were operating on my uncle and he would survive. This was all taking place while two unknown surgeons who happened to be available performed intricate emergency surgery on my uncle.

Grandma was praying to Saints Cosmas and Damian for their intercession. These two saints were doctors. Shortly after this occurrence Grandma developed, what some might consider, unusual spiritual gifts including prophecy. It always amazed me how her bedroom looked like a mini-church, complete with candles, statues, and many prayer books. When I visited her after school, which was a block away, she would immediately bring me into her room and read stories of the lives of the saints. It fascinated me. All the while, during some of our visits I noticed some of these "saints" appearing in the room. They would smile at me and put their hands on Grandma's shoulder.

She had a large picture of St. Michael the Archangel slaying the dragon. I remember my cousins used to say how afraid they were to go to Grandma Pokey's because of all the spooky stuff she had at her house. I was not afraid, I was comforted. These were familiar faces to me. Somehow I knew Grandma knew that I was aware of these beings. During these story sessions I could see myself in the scenes that were taking place. When she read me stories of Jesus and Mary, somehow I felt I had already experienced and knew these loving people.

Let me just say, I was all of seven years old when this was happening to me. She was also a devout Catholic and attended Mass daily. If I were visiting with her for longer periods of time, we had to go to Mass first, and then off to the five-and-dime for a sandwich and ice cream. Whenever I was with her and especially at Mass, I knew I was safe and able to relax. Grandma with the candles, as my nieces and nephew referred to her, was the one person I could curl-up with and be myself. I loved her dearly.

When I was about four we moved from New York to California. My sister RoseMarie (Ree) is fourteen years older than me and we were very close. She was my other mom, so to speak. Ree wrote about me in her diary as always speaking to my Angel and becoming upset if anyone interrupted me. I named my first doll, Angel. She sits on my bed till today.

This was my normal. There was no reason to think otherwise. Ree moved out of the house and got a job while we were still living in California. I was devastated. My sister and best friend moved away. I never forgot how empty this made me feel. However, my wonderful companion, my Angel was there to comfort me.

By the time I was six and a half years old we all moved back to New York. My parents, Ree and my brother Bernie were all together again. Life was good. Shortly after we moved back I had a life altering experience with a man who worked at the park. I became a statistic. I was a victim of child molestation. My parents immediately moved to the Castle Hill area in the Bronx.

However, the impact followed me. I became secluded, shy and distrustful of adults. We lived in a very small attic apartment and I remember crying out to a statue of the Virgin Mary. I felt as though no one heard me. Then the unimaginable happened. Mary appeared to me. She was dressed in a light blue gown with a white veil. She was surrounded with a gold iridescent aura. Her hands were small and she reached out to me to take my hand.

Through my tears, I could see other figures behind her but was unable to identify them. However, I was not afraid. She told me that she would always be with me and not to be afraid. I asked her why the man hurt me.

All she said was, "He is not going to hurt you anymore".

I looked at my hand in hers and felt as though she was the only person I could trust. The amazing colors and light that flowed from her hand into mine was something I cannot describe. She said she loved me and that I would never be alone. I believed her. I knew my life was never going to be the same and it was not. Other than attending St. Helena's school, I had no interaction with many children.

Within this attic apartment, there were secret (or so I thought) hiding places I could go to and have full-blown conversations with my spiritual companions. Who needed human friends? There was a younger girl next door that I associated with, but I would rather go to Grandma's house and visit with her. By the time I was eight or nine years old we moved again to a different part of the Bronx on Waterbury Avenue. This time I had my own room and where I could retreat to play and study. All the while thinking my mother was totally oblivious with whom I was communicating. Guess what? I was wrong. Mommy knew.

When I look back at that time in my life, I now realize those alone times were really a time for developing greater relationships with these spiritual beings. Truthfully, my grades were not that good and my mind seemed to be preoccupied with thoughts that were more important than school. Be assured that did not fly with the nuns at St. Helena's, especially Sister Margaret Mary. Wow, she was a tough one.

The apartment we lived in was only about a block and half from Saint Raymond's Cemetery, which was probably the largest cemetery in the Bronx. Many, many times I was drawn to go into the cemetery and just walk around and talk to whom ever was there. Don't get me wrong, I was not seeing ghosts; I was seeing Angels, saints, and other beings.

As a kid, there was no way in hell I was thinking, *Yep, I'm talking to ghosts*. No one really knew I was frequenting St. Raymond's. My thoughts were, *Why should I say anything?* Again, I believe this was my training time for what was to happen in the future.

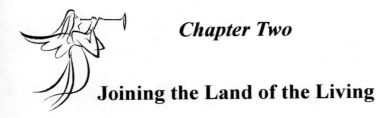

Chapter Two

Joining the Land of the Living

By the time I was finishing sixth grade at St. Helena's, I was almost failing in all my classes, except Religion . . . no kidding. My parents were talking about moving and I was thrilled. My brother is eight years older and was drafted into the Vietnam War. My mother was beside herself. Maybe by moving, we could all start fresh, at least that's what I was thinking. Thankfully, we did it.

We packed up and moved to Upstate New York. It was Piermont, all of forty-five minutes from the Bronx. The family thought we were practically in another country there was so much drama. This was the absolute best thing that could have happened to me. New friends, new school, new home, and no one knew anything about me.

This was heaven. My parents reluctantly enrolled me in public school with the promise I would work extra hard academically. This was easy. I was ready. My grades went from being in the toilet to honor roll. Who knew? Friends were made and puberty began. My thoughts went from hanging with my Angel and other companions to boys, boys, and more boys. All this was happening simultaneously and it was confusing the heck outta me. I would hear my Angel tell me that someone was very down today, perhaps you can offer a kind word and let them know they are not alone. Yea right. That's not happening. No way was I going to jeopardize all the good that was going on in my life.

My answer to that was, "Why don't you tell them?"

So little by little I broke away from my time with my spiritual companions. Sure, I knew they were still there, but finding a boyfriend and all that good stuff was far more important and I told Jesus, "Please, no more. I just want to be normal."

Junior high came and went and high school began. Just when I thought it couldn't get better, the bottom fell out. My parents, once again told me we were moving, this time to South Jersey. Yes, that is New Jersey. It may as well have been Istanbul as far as I was concerned.

It was sophomore year and here I am starting in a new school knowing no one. My mother and I became best friends. We went to movie marathons together and worked like crazy to get me into great shape. While being a recluse, I discovered eating as a means of comfort. At sixteen I needed to lose about 35 pounds. With not a whole lot happening in my life except crying, I decided to diet and exercise like crazy. There was definitely a presence with me during this awful time. But because of my own will, I saw nothing. Low and behold after a year I was a sleek 118 pounds. Now I was ready to face the world.

I remember Daddy coming to me and saying, "I found a better job, so we will be moving to North Jersey by September."

I did not know whether to laugh or cry. This would be the third high school and I was only a junior. But, with my new svelte body and good grades I was sure I would meet the perfect boyfriend. At sixteen we moved to Blairstown, New Jersey and life took on a whole new meaning. I met my first love and we dated for three years.

I enjoyed learning to play guitar and all the amazingly fun things teens do. No one told me that when you have all these great moments in your life and learn to trust another human being, sometimes you leave yourself wide open to hurt. We broke up and I thought I was going to die. I can recall crying and asking God to let me hear my Angel again so I would not feel so alone. Nothing, nada, zip. Maybe God was really ticked off at me. Who could blame him? I was given a gift, and I threw it back in His face. Who would ever believe me that I was sorry? Grandma, that is who.

I drove myself into the Bronx to see Grandma. I knew she had all the answers.

"Poppy (that's my nick name)," she said, "God loves you very much and He wants you to be happy. Your time will come when that happiness will be deeper than you can imagine. When you are mature enough to handle what He has in store, you will know."

After that she began speaking in Italian and I did not understand a word she was saying. I went home feeling dejected. I thought, *Why not now*??? Grandma knew that my heart was in pieces and she in her wisdom, only gave me enough information to keep my hope alive.

When I got home, my mother saw that I had been crying, again, and as lay on my bed wondering whether life was even worth the trouble, Mommy came in and lay down next to me and said, "Turn to your Angel, Poppy." This hurts so much right now but you are not alone." For sure, Mommy understood.

We took another move, only this time it was across the country to California. At that point I guess I was ready for a big change. We moved in August of 1978 and in November I was turning twenty-one. Immediately I got a job working for a big Savings & Loan in Beverly Hills. After training to become a credit evaluator in the mobile home department, I came to realize that helping people live their dreams to own their own place, made me feel good. The only thing that kept me sane was thinking maybe this was a second chance at finding some happiness.

My prayer life at this point was slim to none. On occasion I would attend Mass but found my connection with God was more powerful at that time, by the ocean. Most times I drove to Santa Monica beach to stare out into the vastness. God knows I knew He was real, He heard me call out to Him so much, that I kind of felt like He was covering His ears. I was wrong. By the time winter rolled in, I had met a guy whose mother lived in the same apartment complex as my parents and I. He was three years younger and very nice. We began to date and before I knew it he had asked me to marry him.

On July 29, 1979, I got married. We struggled at first, but then settled in to life and actually became active in church life. In January1980, my Mom got a phone call that my beloved Grandma was very ill. By January 31st, Grandma had been taken home to heaven. She was 83 years old. My heart was broken, but I knew she would find a way to stay connected to me forever. In March of 1980 I found out I was pregnant. It felt as though Grandma's spirit would live on in this precious new baby. This was the best gift God could ever give me. The only problem was that I was transferred into collections and the stress level to get people to pay their loans was taking its toll on me.

At six months pregnant I developed extreme gallbladder pain that forced me to make a decision. Either I have my gallbladder removed and risk losing the baby, or tough it out. I chose to tough it out. Thankfully, I went on temporary disability to keep some of my income. My due date was December 10th. Lo and behold, on December 10th the most amazing baby boy was born, my son Michael. When I looked into his beautiful eyes and held him for the first time I knew he was very special. His spirit was familiar to me and for the first time in a very long time, I could feel the presence of a strong Angel, Mary and even more extraordinary, Jesus Himself. That feeling has never left me.

Unfortunately, I was very sick since I had lost a lot of blood and was extremely weak. Michael seemed to be fine until a couple of weeks after we were home and he became very sick. It was one illness after another until finally the doctors told me he was very dehydrated. They were unable to find the cause of all his symptoms and he needed to be hospitalized. They warned me he was extremely sick and was unsure if he was going to pull through.

Michael had IV's in his head, he was pale, and losing weight. *Please God don't take my baby* was all I could think. *Take me, not him.* It was around three in the morning and I was exhausted trying to rest in a chair next to Michael's crib when an older woman with a newspaper and magazine cart entered the room. She saw me standing over the crib holding Michael's tiny hand. She never asked me if I wanted anything, she cradled his face in her hands and she said, "He is going to be alright, don't worry. God hears your prayers."

At first I thought, that is very kind of her to say that. Within minutes I sat down and fell asleep. In the morning it had dawned on me how odd it was that this woman would be coming around at three in the morning. Deep in my soul I knew an Angel had visited us. As of this moment, to me, that Angel was Michael's spiritual companion I had known all along was with him. Michael survived.

Chapter Three

Baby Come Back

Michael spent the first few months of his tiny life sick. It was awful never knowing what was going to happen next; in and out of doctor visits and emergency rooms was the norm for the first three months. At 23-years old, I wondered if I was ready for motherhood . . . too late.

Michael was special in so many incredible ways and I was finding out every day what a spirit-filled baby I had. Amazingly, through all of the illness he was still a joyful little Angel. The connection I had with him was more than what was just a normal mother and son relationship. It felt as though he could look into my eyes and I in his and read each other's thoughts. What I am sure was happening is Michael's guardian Angel and mine were communicating through us to one another. I understand this may sound really strange, but this is a communication that continues today.

By the time Michael was six months old the three of us were moving back east. We wound up in Hackettstown, New Jersey in a two-bedroom apartment. Since there was no way my Mom was going to stay in California without Michael, her little Angel, they followed six weeks later. I thought I had died and gone to heaven. I was home. As life happens, my husband and I drifted further apart. He and my Dad worked together in New York City and all was not paradise.

We separated two weeks before Michael's second birthday. With no job, twenty bucks to my name and no car, I thought I was thrown into a salad spinner. God? Who had time for God? I had to scramble to find full-time work. I was only working part-time at a Dunkin' Donuts and I needed some serious work. Well as God planned it (of course this is all in retrospect) a friend told me of a job at a food broker, and I'll be darn, it came with a company car. Short of begging and weeping, I approached the interviewer with my heart on my sleeve and a boatload of determination. I wanted that job and I was out to prove it. A food broker basically travels from grocery store to grocery store making sure that the products our company represented were properly displayed as well as fully stocked.

Three days later, a phone call came and I was hired. Woo Hoo! Only one obstacle, the car they gave me was a standard transmission and I did not know how to drive it. I told my future boss I would learn by Monday. I was crapping in my pants, so was my Dad, since he was teaching me. Forging forward sometimes means coming to within inches of a brick wall . . . literally. Poor Daddy, I'm sure he did not think he was going to make it out alive. Perseverance proved to work. By the time I started my job on Monday I was driving the Volkswagen Rabbit like a pro. OK, maybe not a pro but at least I made it out of first gear.

As life would have it, surviving means more than just going from day-to-day wondering what is going to happen next. Little by little I began my journey into a new way of approaching life. I am in some control of things and it was my responsibility to do my best and nothing less, not only for myself but for Michael.

As I changed so did everything around me. I was promoted at work to a supervisor, taking better care of my health, and even losing enough weight to compete in a bodybuilding contest. I won for most improved. Yes, I was. It was now time to start thinking about a relationship with someone whom I would be truly happy.

About that time a new guy was hired to work under my supervision. His name was Jerry Reynolds. I heard that Jerry was the son of a guy who worked in the office. I could only think, *So is he to be treated "special"*? This was not going to fly with me. The first time I met him was at the Parsippany Diner on Route 46 in New Jersey. He was all of twenty-two, thin and wet behind the ears. The first thing he asked me was what he should call me. *Like I really wanted to be called Mrs. Anything*? "Sue," I told him. Let's get to work."

I trained him hard and showed him no preferential treatment. It turned out he was a good worker and I actually began to like him. As the year went on we became close friends. About eighteen months into our friendship, we became more than friends. We became a couple, and what a couple of nuts we were.

By October of 1988 we were married. Yup, I married my best friend. Twenty-four years later and we are still best friends and without a doubt soul mates. The cool thing about Jerry is his compassion. Jerry met Michael when he was five. By the time he was eight and a half Jerry adopted him. He has been his Dad ever since and has never looked back. This takes a very special man and thankfully, I am married to him.

Less than a year after we were married we moved to Pennsylvania and the two of us were both commuting into New Jersey. Jerry had gone back to his love of cabinet making for a company in Rockaway and I was with a different food broker. By the time the Spring 1990 rolled around, I knew I could not continue driving all over three states on a daily basis so I took a job at a local newspaper and began a new career.

As an advertising representative I got to meet a ton of people in the Pocono, Pennsylvania area. This job truly suited me. Jerry was also tired of commuting so in 1990 he opened our first cabinet shop, Keystone Custom Cabinets and Woodworks on Route 191 in Analomink, Pennsylvania. This was a huge leap of faith for both of us since Jerry had to leave a decent paying job for the unknown world of owning a business. Daddy and Mommy were right there encouraging us to DO IT!

We had also just built a mother/daughter house. Daddy was battling Emphysema and Mommy had many illnesses herself. This was a really good move for all of us. I will never regret having my parents next door to us. Of course at the time, you do not appreciate what a blessing having those who love you the most right at your fingertips. Like the old saying goes, "you never know what you have until it's gone." Truer words were never spoken.

Daddy worked with Jerry, and I was now manager of *The Pocono Shopper*. Michael was happily growing up around all those who loved him the most. Life was good, or so it seemed. As my job became more and more stressful, I needed ways to release the stress so I started walking. I felt like Forrest Gump at times. All I wanted was to keep on walking. Clearing the cobwebs from my mind during these walks was so important to me.

At the height of all the madness, I was taking my usual walk when I heard a voice say to me, "Get out of the way a car is coming."

I thought, *I must really be stressed out because I am hearing voices.* So I kept right on walking.

Again, "Get of the way a car is coming." By now I was starting to freak out a bit. I started looking around to see if anyone was there. No one was there, at least that I could see.

Something sounded familiar but I could not place it, so I kept right on walking. Finally, I felt a gentle shove push me out of the road and onto the shoulder. Within a split second a car whipped around the curve and missed me by inches. I fell to the ground and was not sure what frightened me more, almost getting hit by a car or the unknown voice. I turned around and headed for home. Jerry was never going to believe this one.

Chapter Four

Milo Who?

Jerry and I talked about what happened and he just kind of shrugged it off as a fluke. However, as the days went by and I walked some more, the voice spoke again and again. I am talking full-fledged conversations. *OK, now I am really losing it and how the heck am I supposed to tell Jerry that his wife is hearing voices?????*

In all this, I knew I had to face the truth, whatever that may be. This voice did not frighten me but comforted me. It did not demand anything of me but spoke as though we had known each other forever. I asked questions and he had answers. OK, Jerry needs to know.

After walking one Saturday morning I decided it was time.

"Jerry there is something I need to tell you. I think you should sit down."

When I began telling him about the "voice", he had what I can only describe as the deer in headlights look. I was not sure if he was going to call the hospital and have me evaluated or just pack-up and leave. He did neither. Instead, he said, very matter-of-factly, "Ask who it is." Heck, why didn't I think of that? Maybe because in my heart I already knew or maybe I was afraid it was some dead relative or something.

The second conclusion was not an option. So the next day I was off walking and there it was again.

This time I had the courage to ask, "Who are you?"

Very gently he said, "I am your guardian Angel sent by God. I have been with your since the moment you were conceived and I will be there to take you home."

Oh no, I thought, *am I dying*?

"No you are not dying."

Whew! That was close.

"So why me? Why now," I asked.

The answer was this, "You are being called to spread a message of hope to many. Let them know they are not alone and that God loves them so much that he has sent guardians to help them through their lives."

No problem, I thought. There have been a multitude of prophets, saints and sages throughout time and Sue Reynolds is going to somehow convince people of this? Are you kidding? Why not some nun or priest?

They crucified Jesus, a kind, loving gentle and innocent man for speaking truth and what makes you think anyone would listen to me, I questioned. Now for sure I thought I was going nuts.

All I could think to say was, "My plate is really full right now and I'm not sure this is right for me."

Can you believe it? The nerve of me. My Angel has a message from God and I am too busy? Really?

God was not taking no for an answer. The messages came daily. At this point I figured it was time to find out exactly how to address this Angel, so I decided to ask his name. To my surprise I saw . . . literally MILO in big block letters in front of me.

Go figure, an Angel whose name means "apple" in Greek. I found that out later. Milo was and still is my constant companion. Of course I was always told that he serves God and so any and all communication was to further my relationship with the Creator.

Can you imagine? My head was spinning. This was the voice I had always heard. This was the Angel who rescued me in a terrible snowstorm as I was sliding backwards in my car down a hill. He showed up just as I was screaming because I could not see two feet in front of me and my car was going backwards towards a ditch. Truly, I thought I was going to die. All of a sudden a guy with a red plaid shirt in a pick-up was coming down the hill on the opposite side of the road. He stopped his truck with no problem and preceded to tell me not to worry, he will push my car up the hill.

My car at this point was at a standstill. He got behind the car and yelled, "When I start pushing, you keep going and don't look back."

He pushed and I hit the gas and started moving up the hill. As I built up enough speed to get over the crest, I turned to wave a thank you and there was no one there. No person, no pick-up truck, nothing.

When I began hearing Milo again, I asked him if he was the man in the pick-up that night. He said, "Yes, God wasn't ready for you yet."

As our relationship grew, my attitude toward God, church, family and even work began to change. Jerry and I started seriously attending church every week and actually wanted to be there.

*   *   *

"The Women Who Changed My Life"
-by-
Deacon Jerry Reynolds

First I want to thank my mother Patricia Ann Reynolds (1937-2010) for being a co-creator with God and bringing me into this world, for giving me a stable home life and especially planting the seed of faith in me. "Thank you Mom."

My name is Jerry Reynolds and I was raised like any other kid. We had some problems in our family and who doesn't. My mother handed on her Catholic faith to her children; we made all of our Sacraments and went to church regularly. But when my parents split up in 1972 everything changed. My mother found herself with no job, a house to take care of, and to provide for three children. She was working full-time and also found herself having to work on the weekends to make ends meet. Something had to give and unfortunately it was church. I was away from God and the Church for many years. But as I said earlier, that seed was already planted.

The next great moment in my life occurred on July 6, 1986. It was a hot summer morning, the first day of my new job. I had to meet my new supervisor at the Parsippany Diner in New Jersey. We met at nine in the morning. Nothing was out of the ordinary when we met except that I do remember when I first saw Sue. There were no sparks or any other sort of magical connection. I remember

15

showing her all the respect in the world and I wanted to know how I should address her or what I should call her. So I asked, "What should I call you Mrs. McKinnon?"

She just laughed and said, "NO! You can call me Sue."

Sue and I became the very best of friends in a very short amount of time. We were like book ends. Watching out for each other and would confide in one another about all sorts of things, events, and even our girlfriend and boyfriend situations. After we became so close, we started to have feelings that were more than just friends.

We started to date and we fell in love. I think we were already in love with each other prior to our dating, because we were best friends. We eventually got married on October 8, 1988. On June 15, 1989, I adopted Michael, my son. Everything was going great with Sue, our son Michael, and me. Our lives together were fine and what seemed normal. Sue was always a very faith-filled person and by her faith we all started to attend church again at St. Matthew's in East Stroudsburg, Pennsylvania. That was a good thing.

As the years passed I did notice a shift, a change if you will, in our relationship. It seemed that a division was starting to ever so slowly creep into our lives. Sue was being drawn deeper into her faith—a lot more than Michael and I. This was going on for quite sometime. Her prayer life changed and I noticed that she was becoming much closer to God. She became a Eucharistic Minister (distributing Holy Communion) and became a volunteer to help bring communion to the sick in the hospital. She started teaching in CCD (Catholic Catechism) classes and becoming more active in prayer groups and a lot more involved with the church in general. I remember one time she was trying to explain to me how the presence of God was so powerful on the altar when she served at Mass.

She told me how nervous she felt when she was holding the host (communion) or the cup (The Precious Blood of Christ). From my vantage point being out in the congregation it looked like it was no big deal, a very easy and simple task. That is how it looked to me. I thought, *How hard can this be? What is the problem?* This was my way of thinking at that time. Then that is when it hit me. I felt left out, angry because I now felt like I was second in her life. She was all about serving GOD and what she could do for others. This is how that slow separation was happening.

The Day!

Then the day came when Sue approached me and asked me to sit down, she wanted to talk to me. I thought, *Oh no, what is this all about?* I did not know what to think. Then she started to tell me that she was hearing voices. She explained the incident on the side of the road, hearing a voice, and someone or something thing pushing her out of the way so she did not get hit by a car. She kept a lot more incidences to herself and then little by little, started to explain a lot of them to me. I wanted to seem to her like I was supportive and accepting because I knew we were on shaky ground, or so I thought, and I did not want to shun her. That would have been devastating. She was told the voice was her guardian Angel Milo.

The other thing that started to happen after she told me what was going on with her experience with her Angel is that she was able to see and hear messages from God through other people's Angels. This information she received was not by her own doing, and the word started to spread. I guess it was God's will that she was chosen to spread His word. But it did not help us much. I became more disconnected and separated because Sue seemed to be involved more in other people's lives then in mine. I was jealous and envious. Sue was trying to help me as well but I was shutting her out. We would go to church and she knew that I was receiving the Eucharist and I had not been to confession in over twenty years. She kept asking me to go and I would not.

As she kept growing in her faith I felt she was trying to force it on me. I remember one time we got into a huge fight over how I felt she was forcing her ideals, her knowledge, and information on me. I turned around in the heat of the moment and said, something that I should not have said, but it was too late. I said to her that she was turning into a religious nut. A HOLY ROLLER!

After that I knew we were really on shaky ground and something needed to change or our relationship was over. But how could this be? God brought us together. Was it going to be God getting in the way to destroy us? No, it was not God it was me. I knew I needed to make a change and it was not going to be easy. How I could start this process/change? I needed to let go and let God. A lot easier said than done.

Sue kept on using her gifts speaking and directing people to God. She helped so many people find God and also explained to them how their Angels were with them, guiding them and helping them. Sue also kept after me to go to confession and I was not ready. I convinced myself that God already knew my sins so why confess them.

Sue told me, "Confession is not a time for you to talk to a priest, it is a time for God to speak to you one-on-one." She continued to tell me that God works through the priest. He is the vessel through which God works.

How easy it is for us to acknowledge our sins to ourselves but try saying them out loud to another person such as a priest in confession.

She continued telling me, "Acknowledging our sins and saying them out loud makes them real. We actually hear them smack dab in our face."

WOW, she told me that message came from God for me.

I thought, *Yea, OK* to myself. I just kept all this in my heart and I was still fighting not going to confession.

Conversion Day

The day was July 26, 1998. It was a beautiful sunny summer day. Sue and I took the day off from work. It was a Friday and Sue and I wanted to spend the day together to have a three-day weekend. I asked her what she wanted to do. She said with so much excitement in her voice, "Why don't we go to St. Anne's Basilica in Scranton it is her feast day?"

"Are you kidding me?" I said to her, "This is what I took the day off for, so I could do this?" I noticed I was crushing her spirit and I was not living up to what I wanted to do . . . "CHANGE".

So I apologized and said, "OK let's go." We left East Stroudsburg at 12:00 noon. An hour later I noticed as we were going up St. Anne's drive how empty it was. We actually pulled all the way in front. Now the road was at least six to eight car widths wide. We were right up front on the right hand side of the road at a stop sign. I did not think much about it at the time.

We parked the car, got out, and crossed the street to where the festivities were taking place. There were all sorts of booths, food vendors, tents and exhibits going on. I thought to myself, *Wow, this is cool because I love to shop and browse around and look at different things and to eat festival foods.*

Sue and I were just having a wonderful time eating together and looking around. There also was a prayer garden on the grounds and Sue asked me if I would walk it with her to pray together.

I said, "Sure why not."

I can do this with her because it will mean a lot to her and maybe this was the reason why I went to St. Anne's Basilica that day. I was trying to change and hey, this was the first time I did not feel hesitant to pray with Sue and to be with her in this capacity. Things were going great. We ate, and walked around for about an hour and a half. I was now done seeing all of the different things. I asked Sue, "Are you ready to go home or do you want to do something else?"

She said, "Are you sure, I would like to stay." "Let's go I am getting tired," I said, because I really didn't want to stay. When we got back to that road where we were parked, which was empty when we arrived, it was now completely packed. I mean not one space was left. In front of my car at that stop sign was a wooden barricade and a police officer was right near it directing people across the street. I went over to the police officer and asked if he could move the barricade so I could pull straight out. I could make a right turn and be on my way. Well God had a different plan. The police officer said he could not do that and I would not be able to leave until after the novena Mass.

A novena Mass is a celebration that occurs after nine days of prayer. The Mass is the highest form of praise Catholics give to God, to strengthen us for the journey ahead.

The policeman said, "You might as well go into the church and enjoy the Mass."

I said to myself, *YOU KIDDING ME?* This was great, I now have to go to Mass on a Friday. I came here to enjoy the day with Sue and to do some religious stuff with her and now I have to go to Mass too? I was not a happy guy. I knew Sue was filled with joy because she wanted to stay without forcing me into it. Or was she? Were all of her prayers finally paying off? I don't know. But here I was going to a novena Mass in honor of St. Anne. So we went inside.

Now you have to understand, in Scranton, Pennsylvania, there are many devout Catholic Christians. This church was packed to the gills. I mean it was standing room only. Sue and I found ourselves as far back from the front of the church as anyone could be. There was Eucharistic Adoration (where the Holy Eucharist is exposed on the altar and we have the opportunity to be in the presence of Jesus) going on and also confessions at the same time. Inside the church there were at least eight confessionals off to the right side of the church as you were looking at the altar. There were many people waiting in line to go to confession.

Sue leaned over to me and said, "Hey today might be a good time to go to confession." I was steaming inside already because I had to go to Mass and she is after me now to go to confession.

"NO, I am not going. Leave me alone." And that is what she did.

Then something extraordinary happened as we adored Jesus, and people were waiting their turn to go to confession. I did notice one of the confessionals was not being used, because there was no red or green light on that confessional which signals if it is occupied. I was standing in the back of the church and I was right in line of the Blessed Sacrament being exposed. It felt what I can only describe as someone picking me up. I felt like I was levitating two inches off the ground. I had no control of myself and I found myself being lead right over to the confessional that was not being used. But all of a sudden as I found myself in front of the confessional, now the green light appeared meaning I could go in.

I walked inside and sat down. I could not believe this was happening to me! I was scared, confused and excited all at the same time. Then I said, "Bless me Father for I have sinned, it has been over twenty years since my last confession.

In a VERY DEEP but comforting voice I heard, "I know my son I have been waiting here all day for you."

After that this person, this priest was reading my soul. He was telling me all of the things I had done and some of the things I had done and had forgotten about. It was truly amazing and I was dumb-founded that he knew all of this. I left the confessional and it was like twenty pounds of bricks were taken off my back. I felt great, reborn if you will, a new person. Everything in an instant was starting to change.

I found Sue and a pew to sit in as I started to do my penance that is a special prayer to remind us of the tender mercy of God. Mass was just about to start. I remember I was keeping an eye on that confessional because I wanted to see the man who read my soul. I wanted to see what he looked like so I could later go to him and thank him. But that never happened. No one ever came out of the confessional and I kept a keen eye on it to make sure I did not miss anyone. No one else went in and no one else ever came out. During that Mass the Holy Spirit revealed to me I just had an encounter with God. It was God in that confessional speaking to me. Speaking to my mind, my heart, and my soul. It was just as Sue had told me earlier. Confession is not you speaking to God, it is God is speaking to you. This is food for our souls to give us strength for the journey.

That was the day that changed my life. Thanks to Sue for being the vehicle God worked through that day. If it was not for God working through her suggesting we go to St. Anne's Basilica who knows where I or we would be today. Three years later I found myself applying and being accepted in the permanent diaconate program and after five years of studies I was ordained as a Permanent Deacon on November 27, 2004. Thanks be to God.

Thanks to Sue, and the rest as they say is history.

*   *   *

Suddenly I felt my job at the newspaper was OK, but I knew in my heart there had to be more. At that point, the secretary at work needed to take an indefinite leave of absence and the position needed to be filled. Daddy had been working with Jerry in the cabinet shop but was rapidly becoming unable to breathe and stand for any length of time. It was then I realized my Dad knew how to type and answer phones so why not have him work at the paper. He did and I loved it. We had many deep conversations during our lunch breaks. These are the times I hold deep in my heart.

There was a time when my protective "Daddy" could not help himself. An irate customer came to the front office and demanded to see the manger. Daddy paged me and as I was coming down the hall to speak with the man and he decided to start walking towards me yelling and screaming obscenities.

Holy cow, my Dad flew out from behind the desk and told that man to "Get the hell out of Sue's face" and escorted him to the front door. The guy left but not before threatening both of us. When everything calmed down I remember telling Dad he did not have to worry because I had Milo with me.

His reply was, "Who?" Perhaps it was time to explain some things to him.

When I did talk about it, Daddy just looked at me and said, "I always knew you were special and speaking to someone. I'm just glad it was an Angel."

Chapter Five

Sickness and Sadness

It was Halloween 1994 and we were having a huge costume party for the entire newspaper employees and friends. We had a contest to see who could design the coolest tombstone. Everyone thought I was going to come dressed as an Angel. Maybe because since I was a child, I collected all kinds of Angel figurines and I always spoke of Angels to everyone who would listen. Did we surprise everyone when Jerry and I showed up as a sorceress and a devil.

My mother was not happy about this choice. She actually was scared and told me not to "play around with the other side." Of course being the stubborn thick-headed Sicilian that I am, I did not listen. The party and contest were successful and not another thought was given to my costume choice.

In my heart I knew that the dark side was very real. It was not just the "good" Angels that I was able to see and hear, but also the "evil" entities that were always attempting to sway me in the other direction. Perhaps I wanted people to see me as having a good sense of humor. Or perhaps, I was truly being led by the enemy. Perhaps it was both my ego and the enemy. Either way it was a lesson I would never forget.

Two days later Michael came down with a high fever of unknown origin. When I phoned his pediatrician and told him about Michael's fever of 104, he told us to meet him immediately at the hospital. Michael was admitted and the doctor was not hopeful.

After pumping him with really strong antibiotics through an IV that could kill anything, Michael was still extremely sick and the fever was not leaving him. A spinal tap was ordered. After a battery of tests, the doctor told us that Michael had a very rare form of pneumonia that generally was not seen in thirteen year old children, there was not much more they could do. He told me to pray.

My parents came to the hospital and Daddy began to weep at the sight of Michael's frail state. At that point Daddy had been in-and-out of hospitals himself. The emphysema was progressing rapidly. I could hear Daddy begging God to spare Michael and take him instead. We all were crying uncontrollably. Jerry needed to go home that night to let the dog out and I decided to stay with Michael through the night. At this point a few words should be said regarding Michael's relationship with my Dad.

They were best buds. They went everywhere together. Daddy took him fishing (Daddy hated to fish), attended all his football and baseball games and especially just loved him unconditionally. Michael adored his Grandpa. As Daddy's disease got worse, Michael would run to help carry in the groceries for Nanny and Grandpa and even help remove Grandpa's shoes. He never once complained about helping his grandparents.

After everyone left the hospital and we were alone, he became delirious.

The fever was spiking and he turned to me and said, "Mommy I'm not going to make it."

It took everything in me not to scream at the top of my lungs, GOD HELP HIM!!

Holding his hand and praying with all my might I finally closed my eyes for about five minutes when all of a sudden I thought someone came in and turned the lights on. I opened my eyes and all I could see were the balloons flying wildly back and forth, a huge Angel and what appeared to be my aunt Margie, who was deceased, were standing on the other side of the bed.

This Angel had his hands over Michael and my aunt was just smiling at me. I could only think, *They are coming to take Michael to God.* I had an overwhelming sense of peace come over me and was not afraid. Within minutes, they vanished and I fell into a deep sleep.

The next thing I heard was Michael saying, "Mom I'm hungry. When is breakfast coming?" The fever broke and I knew Michael was healed.

Thank you God. It was not until years later that I asked Milo who the Angel was that was sent to heal Michael, he said, "Michael's Angel, Daniel." What a blessing.

*   *   *

"My Mom . . . The Angel Lady"
-by-
Michael Reynolds

Have you have ever wondered what it was like to talk to Jesus and have him write His answers so clear on your heart and soul, that you allow yourself to believe his message is meant for you to hear? If this was to happen my first question would be, why and why me?

Answers to questions like this seem easy if your answers are coming from Jesus, but the depth of understanding an answer to a question like this is more than a lifetime deep. It can take a long time to even realize the gift that you have, and an even longer time to trust that these gifts are real. Let alone know what to do with them.

This was no different for my mother . . .

Over time, she has been able to trust in what God has been telling her. God has been speaking to her through messengers like Angels, Saints, Mary, and Jesus Himself, to write His understanding on her heart and soul. That is an extremely difficult responsibility for any human to bear. It takes a toll on a person's mind and body; I have seen firsthand what it has done to my mother.

When my mom first started to realize that she was communicating with her guardian Angel Milo, I was very skeptical about what was really going on. Almost embarrassed that this was happening to her, I had all the same questions you might in my head . . . *Why, why you, why my mom?*

To this day I do not know the answers to those questions and I do not believe that I will until God is ready for me to know. I do know however, as Mom started to trust in herself and in what Milo was saying to her, the relationship between God and my mother started to grow much stronger. The conversations gave her understanding of what was going on around us and the messages began to come more clearly. She would not let me forget God was trying to speak to me too, and that one day I would be ready to listen. Little did I know at the time, God was already speaking to me through my mother.

As time went on the experiences became more and more real. When people came into the room, right away my mom would be able to have an understanding of their spirit, and what was surrounding it. She could talk about the things only you would know deep in your subconscious—feelings that were only real to you, messages that you needed to hear to give you a better understanding of what you might already know to be right in your heart. You would know it is truth, because God put it there for you. But life buries it away, so you cannot receive it. Mom would uncover that message, because she could hear what God was trying to tell *you*. That's why they call her the "Angel Lady".

We live everyday within two worlds, our lives as we know it and the spiritual world that surrounds us. As you become closer and closer to the Lord, the two worlds can start to become easier to see more clearly. For some reason God has chosen to reveal a deeper understanding of the spiritual world surrounding us to my mother.

As a teenager I fought my own feelings, I allowed the thought of, *All of this can't be actually happening,* block me from hearing what God was writing on *my* heart. I would not let my mind be free, doubt controlled me, and negative thoughts consumed my mind and would not let me go. None of that was from God.

One night I was working late. I was a waiter at a resort during my Senior year in high school, and I had an overwhelming feeling my mother was praying for me, I could almost feel the words that she was speaking. As my shift ended and I got into my car I called my mom to ask if she had been praying for me. That was a dumb question since she prayed for me all the time, so of course she said yes.

I asked her what was she praying for and she replied, "For you to hear God."

That night, I went to an open field at the resort, sat on the hill, and begin to speak to God. Then the words that my mom said kept coming into my mind and I realized I was always doing the talking and I was never waiting for God to answer. God never talked to me that night, but he opened my heart and opened my mind to a different thinking, and a different understanding of the relationship I could have with Him. This experience also helped me believe much deeper in my mother. I always knew she believed this was real and she was not just making this up, but I could not get my mind around if it was coming from God, or from her.

My faith in the Lord and my thirst for a deeper relationship with Him drove me closer to my mother as she continued to be an inspiration in my life and instrumental in the lives of the people she met.

I wanted more and more to dive into the unknown and develop a relationship with God to give me the ability to hear and understand His message. My mother loved it when I made time to be with her to pray. It is the most amazing feeling to feel the presence of Jesus holding your hand or touching your head, delivering His love and opening your heart and mind to the messages He wants you to know. I always said that He would write them on my heart and give me such a "knowing" of His words. But then when my mom would speak the words Jesus had just written on my heart, I was always in awe of the miracle taking place.

See, this might seem strange to some people and I understand that, but for my family this is everyday life. My Grandma had such a powerful gift of prayer, her relationship with God was so strong from a child I remember her intimate conversations with God. As a little boy, I was exposed to a spiritual way of thinking. Growing up with a mother that knew what you were thinking and feeling did not always make things easy, but it allowed me to believe what was happening to me was real.

They say it is easier to not believe in God then it is to believe in Him. They also say the same thing about the devil. The greatest trick of the devil is that he tries to convince you he does not exist. Right? We have heard this lie before.

My mom told me to be careful of whom I listen to, and to always do my best to discern where the message is coming from. She knew when evil spirits were present and lingering around someone. She could find out why or what it was there for and how much it controlled the thinking of the person she was talking to. She can sense evil as it enters a room and battle them on a spiritual level with the power of the Lord on her side, allowing the person to discover for themselves what God was trying to say to them.

It is amazing how evil can clutter your mind with thoughts of doubt and fear, how they can put barriers in the middle of your spiritual path, causing you to trip and fall. This is their purpose, and they are very good at what they do. Life gives evil spirits so many weapons to work with, but nothing can defeat the love of God, so they do whatever they can to distract you from feeling that Love. Mom breaks down those barriers, clears the distractions, and takes on their spiritual punishment herself, all so God can deliver the message He has for you.

As a young man it was challenging enough becoming an adult. But, being exposed to this extremely vivid spiritual world has me turned upside down when it came to discerning what was coming from God or what was coming from the devil. In fact I was getting very good at conversing with evil spirits, I could feel them around me in a room. I would be able to identify their purpose and help to drive them away. I began to feel a sense of power and began thinking I could handle them. I wanted to explore deeper and get a better understanding of how they worked in people's lives. Despite all the warnings from my mother, and all the pleading she would do with me not to dive-in past what was meant for me to handle from God, but I felt confident in my faith and continued.

This led me to be consumed, I started to only feel, see, and hear this evil. No longer could I bring myself to hear what God was writing on my heart, my faith begin to weaken, and doubt started creeping back into my life, shutting me out of the light. Every time I tried to shut it out and pray to God, I was attacked at night in my own bed. My fiancée, now my wife, would wake-up next to me as I was screaming for God to protect me. The room would get very cold and I could feel the evil presence grabbing and pulling at my skin. Then it would stop . . . as if someone covered me with a warm blanket and pulled me out of freezing cold waters. I finally came to my mother for help, and I was scared like a little boy who was having nightmares.

I did not have to say much to her, she already knew what was happening to me. As I was being attacked she would get it ten times worse. She got this torture much more often than me and it was much more physical, but whenever I was being attacked she was too. It was her prayers to Jesus, Saint Michael, and the Blessed Mother that protected us on those nights. She took them on for me, and for many other people as well. Over the years this has taken its toll on Mom physically and continues to everyday. If you are going to call an evil spirit out, expose them, and recognize their presence, then you will attract their attention in a way that you do not want to. That I can tell you is more real than you want to know.

I have been fortunate in my life to have had some of the most amazing people you would ever want to know help me find my way through this spiritual battle ground we call life. As I look back at my journey I can truly say I have been blessed with the love of an incredible mother. She has faced adversity, doubt, fear, and physical torment yet she continues to deliver the message God writes on her heart.

She will describe herself as a vessel for God's message, nothing more . . . But she is much more to me; she will always be a guiding light into a spiritual world that surrounds us every day. She has continued to help me find the Lord and stay in His light year-in and year-out. She will always be a reminder of what is real. Whether in this life or the next, I know she is always with me and I will always have that special connection with her. I love my mother for who she is and all that she represents.

*   *   *

As I mentioned before, my heart was restless being at the newspaper. I needed something more but I just did not know what. The cabinet shop was growing rapidly and we were outgrowing our location. Jerry and I decided to buy a building in Stroudsburg. We met with the realtor who happened to be the son of a very close prayer partner of mine, Ronnie Baxter. Her son Michael was very helpful and told us all about this great building, off the beaten path. My first thought was, location, location, location. Although we were in downtown Stroudsburg about a block off of Main Street, it felt like we were in the middle of nowhere.

This did not seem like a good idea to me. Jerry loved it. Oh no, conflict. Jerry asked me to ask Milo what we should do. Of course he knew I could not just summon him whenever I felt the urge, but to placate him I went into a small office space and began to pray.

Truthfully, I was hoping Milo would not show up. So much for what I wanted, Milo was there and eager to respond. "Milo, is this a good place for us to buy, I asked?"

His reply was, "Have no fear, this building will be used to glorify God in many ways."

What? This can't be, I thought.

Now I have to tell Jerry. Do I tell him the truth or say Milo was busy? Guess my conscience won out. I told him what Milo said and Jerry was delighted. By December 1994 we owned a building.

By January Jerry said, "Sue you have always loved Angels, why not open an Angel store? You can still work at the newspaper and do this part-time."

What a great idea! Why not? So I began what was named, *Calling All Angels*. Guess what? The store was eventually located in the same room I asked Milo about the building. This must be what he meant. The cabinet shop was up and running and we were planning our opening. How about St. Valentine's Day? Great idea.

Three weeks before the opening Daddy was to come and check out the new place. We were so excited that my parents were going to see the new place for the first time. Unfortunately, by the time Daddy got to the first step, he became so out of breath he could not go another step. My heart was broken because I had remembered him saying at Christmas time that all he wanted was new lungs.

Something or someone told me Daddy would never see the inside of the building. On the day of the official opening of *Calling All Angels*, February 14, 1995, we had to call the ambulance to come to the newspaper. Daddy could not breathe and was turning blue.

As they wheeled him out he looked at me with his beautiful blue eyes and said, "Poppy I am not coming back. If they put me in the hospital, I will die there."

Of course I told him he would be OK, but deep in my soul I knew he was right. The words he prayed beside Michael's bed in the hospital just that past November kept coming back to me. Daddy was taken to the hospital and put on a ventilator. The doctor said it was a matter of time.

My hero was losing this battle and there was nothing I could do about it. Daddy was not going down with out a fight. He wanted the tubes out and wanted to speak to us before he died. The doctors loaded him up with all kinds of steroids and other meds but told us to prepare to say our goodbyes. We called in our pastor, Monsignor John Bergamo from St. Matthew's Church to give Daddy his last rites. As they pulled the tube from the ventilator out, we braced ourselves for the worse.

Mommy was an absolute wreck, naturally. After about five minutes Daddy said he was hungry and wanted a tuna fish sandwich. Could this be another miracle? For us, any time with him was a gift. Daddy was moved to a regular room and we were hopeful. However, the doctors still warned us that he did not have long as there was little or practically no air movement in his lungs.

Let me just say, from February 14th, the day Daddy was taken to the hospital, I was unable to hear Milo. I prayed. I begged and pleaded. Nothing. *Was it happening again? At my worst moments was God abandoning me?* The next few weeks were torture. Mommy stood by Daddy's side and barely ever left him alone. Jerry had asked Mommy to go with him to the cafeteria for a cup of coffee. I stayed with Daddy and welcomed the time alone with him.

Not long after they left Daddy sat straight up and began to tell me that there was an Angel standing at the end of his bed. He knew that this Angel was there to take him home, but he just was not ready.

Daddy also said, "Poppy, your Milo is standing right next to you."

Of course all of this was very hard to take in, but I let him continue without interruption.

He went on to say that he would never leave without saying good-bye to me. He was worried about Mommy and did not want her there when he finally went to God. She would put up a fight even till the end.

"Poppy," he said, "I just need to be by myself."

"Daddy, please don't say you want to be by yourself! We want to be with you." He just smiled and we hugged each other and cried like babies. My hero, my Daddy was leaving us soon and I was not ready.

It was Wednesday morning, March 22, 1995 at about 7:30 and Michael had already left for school. Jerry needed to get to work so he went downstairs to get Mommy and head to the hospital to see Daddy. They had just left the house when all of a sudden as I was putting on my make-up, I heard Milo. I was scared. It was not because I heard Milo call my name, Susan, but because he told me Daddy was there and wanted to speak with me. I began to hold my hands over my ears and say, "La, la, la, la," like a child. I felt Milo touch my chin like he always had done to let me know he was present. That is when I stopped and listened.

Daddy said, "I promised I would never leave without saying goodbye Poppy. I love you and I always will. I can breathe." Just as he finished, the telephone rang.

It was the nurse at the hospital calling to tell me that Daddy had just passed away. He was only 72 years old. All I wanted to do was crawl back in bed and die with him. But, I knew I had to somehow get to Mommy before she walked into his room and he was already gone. I grabbed my purse and flew out the door and drove like a maniac. What was normally a twenty minute ride took me about fourteen minutes. Just as I was approaching the road the hospital was on, I saw Jerry's car. Immediately I started blowing my horn and turning the headlights on and off to get his attention. Thankfully, he saw me. Through the rearview mirror I saw the awful look on his face. We pulled over and I was able to tell Mommy the love of her life for the past 54 years had gone to God.

It is a strange feeling, emptiness. With all the voices surrounding me, all I could feel was empty. How could we tell Michael? Jerry went to his school and picked him up and brought him to the hospital to say his goodbyes to his best pal. Even though it felt like Milo had left me, he stood right by me and opened the veil so I could hear my Daddy one last time.

Thank you my wonderful Angel, thank you.

Chapter Six

Amazing Grace

After Daddy passed away it was becoming very difficult to continue to work at the newspaper, especially since I could see where Daddy sat at his desk, through my office. Changes were taking place throughout the company and the writing was on the wall, I had to start looking for other work. A client friend of mine suggested to one of our competitors that he should give me a call about a job.

At first I was very surprised to hear from this man, but then, I thought, maybe this is a sign. Although Milo never actually said anything, I felt his presence very strong during the conversation. I decided to meet with the gentleman from *Clipper Magazine*. By this time the Angel store was up and running and growing more than I could have imagined. It felt as though I was burning the candle at both ends so Jerry and I had decided that perhaps I should only work part-time for the magazine and the rest of the time at *Calling All Angels* and Keystone Cabinets. As it turned out, that is exactly what happened.

This was the perfect solution for my situation. In May 1996 I began my new job. The Angel store was becoming very popular and since I knew a lot about advertising, I plastered the area with ads. After a year, we were really enjoying our store and cabinet shop, however the clientele was beginning to look for more than just Angel figurines, they came in looking to speak with the "Angel Lady". Yep, that was me.

It seems as though while people were shopping at the store, I would get intense messages from Milo about them. Many times it was because they had lost someone close to them and they were grieving. Many times it was a warning or a message about their health, there were so many messages that I began to feel as though it was my responsibility to pass them along. It was strange at first, speaking with complete strangers because I was never sure about their reaction.

Thankfully, most were very receptive and apparently comforted. Most times I could not even remember what I was saying to them. It is as though the message was made available for the person and then I just forgot it. This is really a blessing since I think my head would explode from all the information. Many times folk would come in and I could see figures standing with them. I asked Milo who they were and many times there would be other Angels, saints or unknowns. It started to become very apparent to me this was a calling from God that I could not just turn my back on.

The first time I told someone how many Angels were with them, I almost had to shake my head in disbelief. I could see amazing lights around people. Many times I could count them and know they were all Angels. Milo would tell me how many were with people and why they were assigned to them.

For example, a friend of mine Kathi, asked about her husband Al since he was becoming a deacon in the Catholic Church. She had come to visit me at the store one afternoon and immediately I knew that Al had his guardian Angel as well as an academic Angel with him. I told Kathi this and she just stared at me with this amazing smile on her face. Afterward she told me that Al was having second thoughts about becoming a deacon because he was afraid he could never compete with the more studious candidates. After hearing he had these Angels with him, he was not afraid anymore. Al is a Deacon today.

Each day I was blessed to have so many encounters with my spiritual companions. I say companions because as I grew in my faith and my spiritual life took on a whole new meaning. My prayer life became so important to me. Connecting with God and being filled with The Holy Spirit was the only way I could stay focused on the mission . . . to bring these messages to a hurting world. Being at Mass and receiving Holy Eucharist was critical for me.

I remember the first time I saw Monsignor Bergamo holding up the host (communion bread) at the consecration and seeing a burst of brilliant light shining over the entire altar. It was as though the host was on fire. It stunned me but something inside of me changed. Deeply, it occurred to me that my life was not my own anymore, but truly belonged to Jesus. He was guiding me. He sent Milo to me and wanted me to continue to trust Him. A few years back, I could not have done it, now I could.

Each day He was strengthening me and filling me with amazing revelations. I began to ask Milo to ask Jesus how to handle people who were not Christians or who had no apparent faith at all.

Milo said, "You must ask Jesus now. You must communicate with Him as you would me. He wants to speak to you."

Wow, I thought. I had come so far and now I was shaking in my boots. This was more than just a prayer; this was a full-blown relationship. I knew that my Protestant friends always spoke about a personal relationship with Jesus Christ and I was sure that was exactly what I had. But this was way more. This was a one-on-one conversation that began to materialize.

My heart wanted this more than anything, even though I knew I was a sinner and totally unworthy. I also knew that what was happening was very, very real. Once again I was faced with the question of how to explain this to Jerry.

By this time he was running the cabinet shop, had three employees and a tremendous amount of work. It felt as though I was going to have to deal with these apparitions, locutions, and visions totally alone. By the way, the answer that Jesus revealed to me about dealing with other beliefs was this, *"They are all my children and they all are here for a reason. Let them know they are not alone. My name is different to many people, but who I AM remains the same. You must know and love me intimately so you can love each person because I AM within them all."*

Not always an easy task, but when I reflect on who told me this, I can not help but want to love. Once, when I called out to Jesus to save a soul I was concerned about, he told me, *"I AM the one who saves, you are just on the rescue mission."* If my ego was ever getting in the way, I have to think of those words and put it all in perspective. Never questioned that again.

In July of 1996, Mommy began to have severe pain in her upper stomach and back. It was determined that she was having gallbladder issues and the gallbladder needed to be removed. As was protocol, we went for some pre-op tests. Keep in mind Mommy was a diabetic and suffered with various ailments. After the tests, the doctor determined she had a far more serious condition that had to be addressed—a heart problem.

We took her to St. Luke's hospital and she was going to have a simple Angioplasty, or so we thought. The heart doctor came out of the room after the procedure and told me that it was much more serious than they had imagined. Mommy needed bypass surgery, immediately. When I went in the room to let her know what had taken place, she was not thrilled about having heart surgery since she only complained about the gallbladder. She also was still very distraught over losing Daddy and really did not care much about living.

After saying a prayer, and suggesting Daddy would want her to take care of herself, she agreed to the bypass surgery. My heart and Milo assured me she was in good hands. The following day we waited anxiously as the surgery was being performed. The doctor assured us she was going to feel much better. We once again gathered in prayer and lifted Mommy up for healing. Ten days later she was released from the hospital good as new, or was she? We brought her to her favorite spot outside her vegetable garden and were reminded of how many blessings God had given us.

About an hour later, less than twenty-four hours after being released from the hospital, Mommy was running a 102 degree temperature and it was back to the hospital.

As it turned out, the only artery they could use for the bypass was the one attached to her sternum, the breastbone. All the other arteries were not usable because they were destroyed as a result of the diabetes. The sternum began to die because there was no blood supply. Mommy had a severe infection in the bone and it had to be removed. Another nightmare was unfolding. After multiple surgeries, intense therapy and over two months in the hospital, Mommy finally was released. I must add, she was never the same.

We spent some time reflecting on all the changes happening one evening, and Mommy said, "I'm very tired Poppy. I don't think I have too much time left."

This till today left such an impression on me. In my heart she was given a second chance and yet she still wanted to leave to be with God and her beloved Benny. How do you argue with that? Through it all she remained faithful but without a lot of spunk.

Every Saturday morning we got dressed and went out to *Calling All Angels* with Mommy. She loved being there. I had a guest book filled with prayer requests and Mommy would spend hours praying for all those people. She would love to hear the people ask for me and want me to tell them all about their Angels. Mommy was always as proud as a peacock when she heard me remind people that everything I was able to do was because of the love of God. As a mother myself, I recognized in her the look of satisfaction in the way she raised me. There are so many accounts of how the Angels were able to touch so many lives; I would need many books to relate them all.

One in particular stands out. It was about four in the afternoon and I was wiping down the shelves when I heard the door open and a woman with her little daughter came in. She briefly looked around then asked if she could speak with me. She began to tell me about her husband who had passed away just a couple of months before in a trucking accident. She told me how her then, four year old daughter Sarah was awakened out of a deep sleep and yelled for her to come into the bedroom. She ran in and Sarah began to tell her that an Angel had come to let her know Daddy was in an accident and that he was all right because his Angel had taken him straight to heaven. She was not to worry because he would always watch over her.

The mother was astonished and told Sarah it was just a bad dream, until about a half hour later when the police came to the door. At this point we were all in tears. Sarah heard about my store from an ad on the radio and wanted to see if she could find an Angel that looked like the one she saw the night of her father's death.

What I learned from Sarah astounded me. She told me as her mother was approaching the building, she saw hundreds of Angels sitting on the roof, flying all around the building and standing guard at the front door. She knew immediately that this was where she was supposed to be. She went on to tell me how she now sees Angels all the time and that she knew I did too. This beautiful little girl who was only five years old, spoke with such authority. She knew she had to do what God had asked her to do. She was one of the most pure souls I have ever met. She continued to visit me at least once a year, for as long as we had the store. What she gave me was something I will never, ever forget . . . validation.

*   *   *

"An Angel Named Poppy"
-by-
Louis Grillo

I grew up in The Bronx, New York in an Italian family. Growing up Italian we had strong religious beliefs. My mother and Sue's mother are sisters, both now deceased. Sue and I were born the same year so no wonder we were always very close cousins. Sue traveled a lot due to her father's work, so we did not get to see each other often. But when we had family gatherings Sue and I always seemed to begin our playtime exactly where we left off. We had an amazing connection together.

I was told that when Sue was born the doctor immediately named her "Poppy" because she resembled the poppy flower. She had a round face, vibrant rose-colored cheeks and a rainbow that glittered out of her smile. I mention this because I believe that when Poppy (Sue) was born something was very different. I should say a Blessing was beginning to bloom from that day on. Till this very day the family continues to call her Poppy.

In the 1920's, the poppy flower had a significant meaning during our parents and that doctor's era. I believe somehow the doctor had seen something or perhaps an Angel whispered in his ear that there was something special in my cousin Poppy to give her this name. The meaning of the poppy flower represents ALL that Poppy believes in.

Poppy had followed her heart. She dedicated her life, gave support, food, and shelter to the sick and poor and countless others.

The poppy flower has its own great story. During World War I the battlefields of Belgium had taken its toll by death and destruction. When the earth was overturned, poppy flowers started to grow wild where the war took place. It was so pretty to see such beauty where devastation had taken place. Today the poppy flower is remembered and given to all veterans who are disabled, hospitalized, and those who need financial help. There is even a poem written about the poppy flower.

Poppy indeed has special gifts. I used to visit her in Pennsylvania at the Angel store where I helped. It was amazing because I worked in a fast-paced, five-star restaurant, a tourist spot, where everyone demanded your attention. But working at the Angel store was the complete opposite. There was calmness about this place that was filled with such tranquility. I considered it a breath of fresh air where customers came in to buy and share their stories of their religious beliefs and miracles they experienced.

I remember a woman came in asking to see Poppy and as the woman was speaking, Poppy interrupted and asked out of nowhere, "Have you had your eyes checked?" The woman looked at her strangely and said no.

A few weeks later that same woman came in and said to Poppy, "Thank you so much for asking me about going to the eye doctor. From that visit I was referred to another doctor and found out I had cancer."

I also remember, myself, Poppy and her girlfriend were in a deep prayer, holding hands sitting on the floor. Poppy's body began to sway and the more we prayed Poppy's face began to change, I saw the Lord's face in her. I don't remember who we were praying for but afterwards we all felt the Lord was healing that person.

People from all over the USA were visiting the store because they heard about the Angel Lady and her Angel connections.

Later she opened a foundation, to help the poor and the unfortunate. There she continues to do the Lord's work. Sue dedicates her work in giving, loving and following what the Lord asks her to do.

The Flower of Remembrance In Flanders Fields

A Poem by
John McCrae

In Flanders fields the poppies blow
Between the crosses, row on row,
That mark our place; and in the sky
The larks, still bravely singing, fly.
Scarce heard amid the guns below.
We are the dead. Short days ago
We lived, felt dawn, saw sunset glow
Loved, and were loved, and now we lie
In Flanders Fields.
Take up our quarrel with the foe:
To you from failing hands we throw
The torch; be yours to hold it high.
If ye break faith with us who die
We shall not sleep, though poppies grow
In Flanders Fields.

*   *   *

"My Angelic Aunt"
-by-
Christina Svolos

When I was about thirteen, my aunt and uncle were visiting our family from Pennsylvania one weekend. We did not get to see them much because of the distance and when they came over, we enjoyed their company to the fullest extent.

I saw my aunt talking to my mom in the dining room and that was when they called me in there. I knew something was going on. For some reason, I remember feeling like my aunt was going to give me a surprise, but I also thought other things could have happened as well.

My aunt wanted to talk to me privately in my room about something important. I did not know what she was going to tell me going in there. Once she closed the door and sat on my bed, my thoughts were all over the place. Was I going to live with them in Pennsylvania for a year? Was she going to give me a sermon on her thoughts about God? She is a very faithful, dedicated, an intellectual woman, and my uncle is a deacon. I had no idea what to expect. All I could feel was the sensation of the unknown.

We were both sitting on my bed, facing each other. The sun was illuminating through my blinds above my bed. I felt almost as if I were in a chapel. My room had turned into a sacred space, but why? Was it because my aunt and uncle were religious so I automatically got the sense I was in a church setting? No. This was something bigger than that. The feeling was different. My room felt almost like Heaven. It was the beautiful sunlight bouncing off the walls that gave the hint I was not just in an ordinary place. I knew it was my bedroom, but it had more meaning behind it now that I was sitting there with my aunt. I knew I was safe and I was able to completely shut-out all other parts of the world. I could reflect and not worry about anything.

"Christina, breathe deeply and close your eyes," she started talking to me like I was going to meditate.

"OK," I said before taking in a deep breath. I was anxious and ready to find out what was going to happen.

My aunt sat on my bed continuing to guide me through what she was doing.

"I see Jesus sitting next to you. He's watching over you and His arm is around you," she reassured me.

"He is?" I said with awe as my heart started to beat faster and I felt that this was a moment so surreal.

"He is with you at all times," she paused, "He is going to touch the right side of your face, okay? Keep your eyes closed and breathe," she further instructed.

My heart started to thump louder. In the two seconds I had to think about what she had just told me, I was honestly shocked. At first I did not think I would feel anything, until Jesus did exactly as my aunt said he would. Jesus touched the right side of my face. It felt like spiritual particles were imprinted on my face.

"Whoa! That's so creepy," I blurted out as it was the first thing that came to mind. I did not think the fact that Jesus was with me was creepy. I thought the fact that it *actually* happened was weird. I never knew something like this could ever happen.

"Don't be scared. He doesn't want you to be freaked out," she spoke slowly and tried to calm my jittery nerves.

Her light Pennsylvania accent was comforting. Now the chapel and Heaven setting made sense. Why did I think I was in a chapel before I even thought about Jesus being next to me? I had a special link to my aunt and God that no one else could understand.

This was real. It was not my aunt's hand either. This was not human flesh. It was Jesus' soul touching mine. I almost felt like His hand went through my face, and this was how he connected with my soul—my inner being that gave me life. This was a connection that sparked through the angelic hand he laid on my face. This is what led my relationship with Him to become much stronger.

I felt sensations inside of my mind, body, and soul. Every part of me was experiencing different things at the same time. My mind was bouncing thoughts off my brain, my body was a little shaky from all my neurons firing twice as fast, and my soul was simply enlightened. It was the most uplifting experience I will have with me for the rest of my life. It is one thing to say that you have been touched by God, faithfully, but I was touched spiritually—I do not think I can really say physically.

We went out to dinner at Sierra's Mexican Restaurant with my aunt and uncle that night. My aunt told me she saw Jesus with every person at the table we were eating at. God really could be everywhere at once. He really does love all of us. The phrase, "God is always with you" was taken to the next level for me.

It hurts me to hear people say that He is not with us when we need Him most because it is not true. Whether or not you choose to feel the presence of God is completely up to you. That is why we have so many different religions in the world.

After this sacred and most special encounter with God, I started living differently. I thought of God in different ways and did not question His existence. The biggest obstacle was posed from those who believed God did not put us here. We sure as hell did not all get here because of the Big Bang Theory. How He put us here and how He put himself here are gifts we will find out when we enter the Kingdom. For right now though, I will keep the knowing that He is always with me. I experience the same sensations in my mind, body, and soul all over again when I feel alone. God is with me always.

Writing this at eighteen now, and in my last 'teen year', I know I am transitioning into a beautiful person because there are people like my aunt and uncle in my life. I have always been told I have an old soul and I believe it more and more every day. I have been touched by God, and I will carry His voice where it cannot be heard.

*   *   *

"The Angel At My Door"
-by-
Artie Conquest

I met Sue in 1997 when I was in my second year of college. I was out one afternoon and decided to check out *Calling All Angels*, I walked in to a room filled to the brim with religious goods, then out through the door Sue came to greet me, I said hello and instantly knew there was something special about her, I did not know what it was just yet, but I knew it was good.

I looked through the stuff in the store and of course purchased many things, and as I was being checked out, Sue looked at me and said, "Our Beloved Mother Mary was very close to me and that our relationship is strong and growing." She also said, that the voices I heard and the things I saw were not me being crazy but the Angels, like many in her store, my jaw dropped open and I left the store in complete awe.

You see, I had never said anything to anyone at that point. A few days later I returned to the store and again bought more items and got to spend a little time with the woman known as "The Angel Lady", we laughed, and talked about New York and many other things. She handed me a prayer card and said she was told to give it to me.

A couple of years later as the store began to grow, so did the news about Sue and her gift. I started to work with her in the store and it was the best place in the world to work because it was peaceful. I always felt a presence there. Sue and I were downstairs unpacking boxes one day and she said that Milo had a message. Milo said that my dad was with me all the time and that he finally made it to heaven, he took a little detour but made it nevertheless.

He said to Milo, "Tell Artie to look for me when he sees the Angels at the tabernacle." I had no idea what that meant, but OK.

As the conversation continued, Sue told me some very personal things that she could never know on her own if it were not for the Angels. She began to tell me about my own gift and that Milo wanted me to meet my Angel named Carmen, AKA Angel of Music. I began to learn from Sue how to talk to the Angels and read their messages, and to figure out what was their voice and what my own voice was.

We had many great experiences working together. One evening we were decorating the store for Christmas and while I was putting the nativity together and every few minutes the phone would ring, I'd stop, get up answer the phone, and nothing. This happened about ten times along with the door buzzer—which by the way was up a flight of stairs. After about forty-five minutes, Sue came in laughing. She said the Angels are giggling because they keep saying, *Look what we can make Artie do*. Then the phone rang once again and I finally realized that they were trying to get my attention so I could speak to them. Hey, I was very new to all of this.

As I was learning through Sue and going with her on visits to schools and classes I was reading every book on the subject. She told my aunt that a woman with blondish hair was with her with the most piercing blue eyes, that was, my grandmother on my father's side. You might as well have given my aunt a million dollars because she started to cry "happy tears" and then talked about her Angel Lady experience all the time up until the day she died nearly ten years later.

I never forgot Sue, as our lives took us in different directions I always remembered what Sue taught me, how she mentored me and how I was able to model my life after her as a wonderful Christian example.

I have this gift and I did not know what to do with it until I met "The Angel Lady" and even today more than a decade later I still check in with Sue to talk with my dear sister in Christ. She and Milo have such an important role in my life that I will never forget them. I have since lost my mother as well as my aunt and if it were not for Sue teaching me how to listen, watch and feel without her guidance, I would be a terrible wreck. She has provided a human touch to this thing we call the "Communion of the Saints". As far as I am concerned, I will always call "The Angel Lady" Sue my friend and I will always consider her FAMILY.

* * *

As more and more people came into *Calling All Angels*, we began the arduous task of remodeling. It seemed as though religious and spiritual gifts were something being sought after. Angels, saints, inspirational books and music were looked at as a way to bring the peace and calm of the Divine deep to the soul. The world was moving swiftly at the turn of the century and I came in contact with many, many people who wanted or needed to connect with someone bigger than themselves.

One of the most fascinating seekers was a professor at East Stroudsburg University, Peter Roche de Coppens. He taught sociology and was intrigued by the angelic world. When we first met, I could see he was a bit skeptical about the "Angel Lady". After much discussion, Peter invited me to be a guest speaker at his end of the year class.

My first thought was, *How am I to reach college students?*" I prayed deeply about whether to accept this invite. After about a week, I contacted Peter and told him I would be happy to be a guest speaker, as I was reminded of the mission from God. Peter, of course gave me a quizzical look. Two weeks later, I was at the first of many classes.

Initially, I spoke of my connection to Angels as a toddler, then my experiences as I grew older. However, it was not until it was revealed to me the number of Angels surrounding the individual students and what they were there for, that really sparked some interest. All of a sudden these students, who I really did not think wanted to be there, were sitting straight up and listening to every word I said. At that point, I could feel all the pain, sadness, joy, and sometimes utter madness emanating from the students' souls. It was both scary and exhilarating.

*   *   *

"When the Angels Went to University"
-by-
Peter Roche de Coppens, Ph.D.

For 35 years, from 1970 to 2005 I taught at East Stroudsburg University of Pennsylvania as a Professor of Sociology and Anthropology. Now I am a Professor Emeritus and still offer lectures, workshops, counseling to faculty, staff and students, and I continue writing books in three languages together with articles for various magazines and newspapers.

What has distinguished and characterized my life is that, as a social scientist, rather than observing and studying normal, sick, crazy, or successful people I have encountered and studied Saints and Sages in various cultures, races, and traditions. These provided for me a "model" and "point of reference" as well as an unending source of inspiration, motivation, and ideals. What I saw and experienced with them is difficult to describe, understand, and accept because we lack an adequate vocabulary. It has definitely not yet entered our collective consciousness and its cornerstone, science. Yet it exists and has always existed and is part of what I call the "spiritual tradition".

What is this "spiritual tradition" which is truly universal and perennial, that we encounter everywhere and yet which has never been institutionalized, rationalized and dogmatized? Known as the "Primordial Tradition", the "PhilosophiaPerennis", or the "Ageless

Wisdom", it is made-up of the experiences and realizations of men and women, of all races, religions, and traditions, who have accessed the fifth level of consciousness and being! While it has a close relationship with religion, it is by no means identical with religion. Authentic spiritual inspiration and experiences have always been the source and matrix of religion, which then, through the work of its clergy and faithful sought to rationalize, institutionalize, and operationalize these insights and suggestions, but which clearly can only reflect the level of consciousness and being of its followers (who are still functioning at the personality level and therefore in the world of duality).

Religion is the "means", it is generally, partisan, exclusive, anthropomorphic, dogmatic, and arrogant claiming to have a "monopoly" on revelation and truth. Spirituality is the "end", and is generally universal, inclusive, non-dogmatic and humble. In all the university courses I have taught in Pennsylvania, nationally and internationally, I have always sought to add the "spiritual dimensions" to the traditional and conventional materials I would present to my students.

For many years, I taught a senior seminar course for sociology students, which is their last course before graduation where I let them choose the topic of discussion and research we follow during the semester. They have to apply the sociological imagination, sociological theory, and methodology, but were free to choose their topic of investigation. One year, in 1998, out of the various topics we considered, one was focused on Angels.

We raised and sought to answer such questions as: Do Angels really exist and are they real? If so what might be their basic nature, distinctive characteristics, essential role, and contributions? Can we study Angels in a rational, academic, and non-religious framework? Can we contact and communicate with Angels and can they make a tangible, measurable, and empirical difference in our lives? How do we explain that most religions believe in Angels and have represented Angels in many statues, icons, images, and legends?

I decided to put together as much information as possible about Angels drawing from a vast literature, several documentaries, videos, and images and stories. I also wanted very much to find a person that had *direct personal experiences* with Angels, for a long period of time, and whose influence and help made a substantial impart in his/her life. I sought, in other words, a person that I could qualify as being *authentic* (namely drawing the information from her own experience rather than from the literature, imagination, or hearsay), who could *distinguish between the psychic and the spiritual realms* (both of which are real and exist but which are quite different), and finally whose life had been substantially affected by this interaction with the angelic realm and that could be studied scientifically.

Someone suggested Susan Reynolds who, at the time, had a shop *Calling all Angels*. I met Susan, interviewed her and was satisfied that she met my basic criteria, and so began our relationship, and how "Angels came to University"!

The first practical thing I did with Susan was to invite her on my university-based TV program, "Soul Sculpture", where I asked her to tell her story with Angels, how it began, and what impact it had on her life and work. We did two one hour interviews after which I invited her to come first to my senior seminar course and later also to other classes as well as I felt she had very valuable, useful, and authentic materials to offer.

Our relationship lasted roughly until 2005 when she moved out of the area and when I retired from regular classes and duties at the university. Thus, I gave Susan about ten TV interviews on "Soul Sculpture" and invited her regularly to my senior seminar and also to other sociology/anthropology classes I taught. Finally, I sent to her a number of people whom I felt she could help, inspire, and guide through her intuition and connection with the angelic world.

Susan told me and then repeated her core stories on our TV interviews. Susan had regular access to Milo, to the angelic world, and spiritual figures who gave her advice, helped her to help others, and told her what the course of her life should be . . . which she was free to follow or not!

For many years, this is what she did. At first I was skeptical but then found out that there were, indeed, many people, the majority being women with children abandoned by their husbands, who desperately needed this kind of service.

At the university, Susan told her many stories with the angelic world and acted as a "clearing house" for her Guardian Angel, Milo, who could interact with the Guardian Angel of a given student and provide very accurate and useful advice. I confess that I have never seen, before or since, so many students really open up and cry as Susan was talking with them. Thus the angelic world had a very deep and measurable impact upon her life and the lives of many others.

When it comes to psychic or spiritual things it is very difficult to ascertain their source as these dimensions and beings can assume any form and shape and use any means and instruments necessary to communicate and have an impact upon the lives of the people they interact with. Thus, rather than quibbling over their religious identity, what scholars and scientists can do is study the effects, the impact and transformations, they bring about in the lives of the people they encounter and touch. This is what I did with Susan Reynolds and which had a profound impact upon my life and the lives of many of my students, and this is how Angels came to University!

On June 12, 2012, Peter went to be with the Lord.

* * *

It felt as though a window was opened into their souls and I was able to view the truths they held close to them. Immediately something changed for me. Emotions that I had never encountered came to the surface. A completely different level of compassion that was deeper and more powerful than I had ever felt was coursing though every fiber of my being. These students were hungry. Hungry for someone bigger than themselves that could direct them when they were feeling lost. There were all different religions represented in these students, as well as those who claimed no religious affiliation. I was not there to convert anyone or convince them that I knew more, on the contrary I felt humbled by the amount of respect they showed towards me and my gifts.

My soul was lifted to another purer and intimate place. I can only describe it as a feeling of oneness with Jesus. It was as though I could understand exactly what Jesus felt when he took pity of those who sought Him out for various reasons, especially when they were overwhelmed with unclean spirits. At this point I should add, the visions of different Angels began to take place.

Let me clarify, I am talking about the not so good Angels. I refer to them as workers of "ole red legs". This may seem ridiculous to some. I totally get that. When I first began to notice evil spirits around people it scared the "you know what" outta me. This dark, empty, negative aura would appear at first and then a full-blown image or many images would materialize. I cannot honestly say what my first thought was, but my instinct told me this was not good—not good at all.

All I can remember thinking was, *I sure didn't sign up for this.* Immediately, when these images appeared, I called upon Jesus. They came close to me but were never able to touch me. I could hear vile, venomous words spewing from their mouths. Sometimes, no words were uttered just an array of awful feelings seemed to silently be sent towards me. The strangest part was seeing the person become directly affected by these entities. Sometimes, the person would break down crying just as I said hello. Sometimes they would almost seem defiant. Whenever I prayed in Jesus' name, the evil would get more violent in nature. Not directed at me, but at the person.

However, I knew that I could not let my guard down during these episodes. My faith had to be so strong because any sign of weakness brought me to a confused and doubtful state. This did not help anyone, least of all the person who was seeking my assistance. These times reminded me how fragile life is and how important it is to stay close to God. Many times in prayer I asked, "Why me?" This seemed like the stuff "Hollyweird" movies were made of. It was time to look for some direction in my life from someone who could understand what I was experiencing as well as guide me. Finding this someone would be a daunting task.

A friend of mine, Helen whose husband was becoming a deacon, recommended a priest named Monsignor John Esseff. I never actually told Helen all that was going on with me, only that I felt I needed some spiritual direction. She seemed to understand without me going into detail. It was be almost six months before I finally got to meet with Monsignor Esseff.

*   *   *

Mark T. Stiles "Angel in My Classroom"
-by-
Mark T. Stiles

My first experience meeting Susan Reynolds is very memorable for me and is something that has always stayed in the back of my mind. I was a student at East Stroudsburg University in 2002 taking a course in Sociology over the summer. The professor for this course is also memorable for me because he was very eccentric and knowledgeable about life and the content he was teaching. I remember one day he informed us that he invited his friend Susan Reynolds to come in and speak to us about some of her stories. He told us she had the ability to see Angels and she was known to many as, "The Angel Lady". This intrigued me right away and I was looking forward to hearing what Susan had to say.

A few days later leading up to Susan coming into our class, something very interesting happened to me. I was over a friend's house and noticed he left a full bag of garbage on his hardwood floor near the front door. When I lifted the bag up to take it outside, I noticed coffee leaked through and left a wet stain on the floor. As I was about to clean this mess up, I noticed something interesting about it. The stain looked like an intricate detailed image of an Angel. I immediately thought of "The Angel Lady" that was going to be coming to my Sociology class to speak to us so I decided to take some photos of this image. This was very ironic and way too much of a coincidence for me.

A couple of days later, Susan showed up to our Sociology class just as our professor said she would. She talked to the class and told us many enlightening stories about some of her life experiences with

Angels. Some were personal and close to her home while others involved random people she encountered. I was amazed at everything Susan had to say and also the type of person she was. I guess when our professor referred to her as "The Angel Lady", I expected to meet someone with extreme religious beliefs who was there to sway everyone toward her way of thinking. This could not be further from the truth because Susan came across very humble and down to earth.

Although Susan seemed like your average everyday person, I soon realized there was something very special about her. After the class ended, I approached Susan to express my gratitude for her coming and I wanted to thank her for sharing her stories with us. I also wanted to tell her about the stained image of the Angel I encountered on the hardwood floor just days earlier. As I walked towards her she looked at me and said in a very sincere tone of voice, "You know that it's all about love."

This caught me off guard, but I paused for a moment and then said, "Yes." After we exchanged these words, I introduced myself and we carried on a regular conversation as though the comment was never made.

For most people, this may seem like a random and odd comment to make to someone you have never met before; however, it made perfect sense to me and it answered something I struggled with my entire life. Since my childhood and into my adult life I always knew there was something different about me compared to my family and friends. For as long as I could remember I always had an attraction to men. As a young boy I did not understand what this meant or why I thought and felt this way, but I knew it was not the norm in society. I tried to suppress these thoughts for fear of rejection and tried to make myself believe that my way of thinking would change as I grew older.

For many years I struggled with this issue and would oftentimes beat myself up over it. I would think about kids in school, people on the news, and religious leaders condemning homosexuality. These people started to make me believe I was a bad person, but in the back of my mind I always had one thought. I always told myself, it does not matter who you are attracted to because it is ultimately about love. On that particular day in class when Susan said in the most sincere tone of voice, "you know that it's all about love", I believe she was reinforcing this one thought that always overpowered my mind when I started to believe I was a bad person.

I reflect on my initial meeting with Susan Reynolds often and I am still amazed at those words she said to me. I think about the days leading up to her coming to my class and how I encountered a stained image of an Angel on my friend's hardwood floor from coffee that leaked out of a garbage bag. My meeting with Susan Reynolds serves as a reminder that there are Angels around us and they are here to guide and support us in our hectic lives. For me these events were never just a coincidence, rather they were a reassurance to what I already knew. It is all about love.

*   *   *

Chapter Seven

The Times They Are A Changing

The talks at the university as well as many other venues began to take place more frequently. At one point Peter Roche invited me onto his local TV show, "Soul Sculpture". Truthfully, I wondered who actually watched local TV, but it could not hurt to be a guest and perhaps plug the store. What I never expected was the flood of calls that came from the first interview Peter and I had.

The weeks after the show aired there were calls and visits to the stores that were unbelievable. There were so many hurting people with so many questions. Poor Jerry would have to keep an eye on the store while I spent time in the area set aide for quiet talks. We both were wearing many hats during the day. I should also mention that we were rapidly approaching the new millennium and tensions seemed to be rising with the Y2K scare.

It was June 1999 when Michael our son graduated from high school and was preparing for college. Michael had a job since he was twelve, delivering newspapers, shoveling driveways, and mowing lawns to make extra money. However, going off to college, working nights and weekends seemed to be a bit much, but Michael felt he was up to the challenge. I was a nervous wreck. This coupled with the fact that my Mom was progressively getting weaker, was making my life seem a bit frazzled.

Michael went off to college in September and decided to live with some friends in an apartment close to the school. This was not something Jerry and I readily approved of since the college was only an hour away from our home and we were afraid of what might happen to Michael once he had a taste of freedom from the parental units. We tried like crazy to convince Michael about all the benefits of staying home, but he would hear nothing of it. He was eighteen and was sure he knew everything. We were just as sure he did not.

Mommy was the most devastated that her "Michael" was leaving, she cried for what seemed like weeks. It was New Years Eve 1999 when Jerry, myself and Mommy spent the evening eating lobster and steak and toasting to the New Year 2000. It was a memorable time on many levels. It turned out to be the last New Year we spent with Mommy. It was also the year I finally revealed all that was happening to me to Monsignor Esseff.

The first time I had met Monsignor I knew I was in the presence of a very Holy man. I attended a healing Mass at his parish and was so completely taken in by his amazing love for the Lord. He was gentle yet possessed a no nonsense way about him. You did not have to guess what he was thinking because he never held back. When the Mass was over and we finally had our first meeting and he blew me away. It was like he knew exactly what was in my soul and could draw out of me stuff I thought was for me alone. There was no way I was going to hide anything from this priest. Believe me when I tell you, that was scary.

He warned me that spiritual direction with him was intense. In his words, this is not a "complain" session, this is a time to learn about what God was expecting of me. Truthfully, I was not sure this was going to be something I could handle. What if he thought I was crazy? What if he thought I was some attention seeker? Who knows what he was going to expect of me? As it turned out, Monsignor challenged me to go deeper into my prayer life, look for Jesus who was within me, and mostly know how much God really truly loved me. When I spoke with him about my Angels, he never seemed surprised. However, he always cautioned me regarding my ego, and not letting it get in the way of God's plan. He also taught me valuable lessons about discerning spirits. He taught me that there are always three spirits at work, our own spirit, The Holy Spirit, and the enemy.

It was Monsignor who encouraged me to become a spiritual director. He felt people needed to be guided even more after they found out about their own guardian Angels. What can I say about a priest who knew St. Padre Pio, was Mother Teresa's confessor and also held retreats for her nuns. This priest was anything but ordinary.

I really wanted to be in his presence so I could learn as much as I could.

In June of 2000, as I was out to dinner with some good friends, LaJoyce and Claudette, when I tried calling home to check on Mommy, however there was no answer. What I did not know was Jerry went home and found Mommy extremely sick. He called 911 and within minutes she was taken to the emergency room. When I finally got home, I thought it was strange that no one was in the house. When I looked at the kitchen table and noticed a note from Jerry, my heart stopped. Within a couple of minutes, I was headed to the hospital to be with Mommy.

When I arrived, a friend, Dr. Nancy Gabana, pulled me aside to tell me she did not think Mommy was going to make it through the night. She had an extreme case of Pancreatitis. At first I was not sure I heard her correctly.

All I could say was, "Nancy you don't know my Mom. She is tough and can pull through anything."

Nancy just reached out to me and held me. Immediately, I went to Mommy and saw Jerry with a scared look on his face. Apparently, he already knew the prognosis. Mommy looked weak, pale, and completely different than from the night before when I last saw her.

She cried and said she was in a lot of pain. We stayed with her until early the next morning as she eventually slept. The doctors put her in ICU and told us it could be anytime. Everything seemed surreal. Jerry and I took turns running home to get a few hours of sleep, shower, and change clothes. Mommy slowly, very slowly began shutting down. It was six days since she was admitted into the hospital and the doctor told me he was amazed she survived as long as she did.

However, it was a matter of hours before her kidneys just gave out. It was June 15th and I decided to stay the night with her. Mommy held my hand and we cried, forgave, loved and prayed throughout the night. When I was a child my mother used to ask me to sing to her. Apparently, I used to love to rock on my rocking horse, Beauty, and sing Italian songs.

At that point I could not remember any of the usual songs, but I knew the words to "Amazing Grace". My voice was barely audible, but Mommy heard me. She never let go of my hand. Even as she slept fitfully, she held on to me. The next morning Jerry came and brought some friends who stood by Mommy's bedside and prayed the Rosary.

Jerry and I went out of the room to speak with the doctor but upon re-entering the room, Mommy removed the oxygen mask and sat straight up and said, "Poppy, look who is here, The Blessed Mother and St. Joseph. You brought them with you."

I knew Mommy was not going to be with us much longer. After we kissed her and told her how much we loved her she lay down and closed her eyes. About noon, she reached both arms up and smiled at Jerry and I. We knew she was on her way to see Jesus and my Daddy.

By 1:15, I noticed her breathing was extremely labored. I held her in my arms and cradled her head all the while listening to her heartbeat getting slower and slower. At about 1:25, she blew out a deep breath and went home. I felt that last breath was her spirit saying goodbye to me.

I became an orphan on June 16, 2000.

Once again, it felt as though someone kept punching me in the stomach, every time I realized neither of my parents were any longer right next door. It is amazing how we take for granted the special moments created each day with those we love until they are no more. An emptiness filled me each day. When Jerry left for work in the morning, I remember walking into my parent's house many times, waiting to hear Mommy shuffle in from the bedroom and say, "good morning". The smell of her delicious cooking was no more. After a few weeks of this, it felt as though we should consider selling the house and moving to a smaller, more manageable home. We discussed it and decided to give it a go. The sign went up and we were on our way to selling the house, or were we? At that time we had two terrific dogs. One was a black lab named Pepper and the other was a Chihuahua named Picolina. Soon after Mommy passed, everyday Pico would run into her house looking for her. Pepper just moped through the day. The strange thing was as soon as we put the house up for sale Pico constantly barked at the clock, for no good reason.

She had never done this before so we thought maybe she was seeing Mommy's spirit.

*   *   *

"My Encounter with an Angel"
-by-
Dr. LaJoyce Brookshire

It was 1995 when I first stumbled into the Angel shop at the end of the road. I had just missed my bus to New York City and I had a two-hour wait for the next bus. I am still perplexed at how I even heard in my spirit "turn here" and obeyed, as there was so much on my mind. I had just returned from a closing to re-finance my mortgage after the death of my husband from AIDS. I was never so glad that I had heard the voice of the Lord and obeyed. He certainly knows exactly what you need when you are in need of it. That day I was the needy.

I entered to heavenly bells and the sight of Angels EVERYWHERE! A bouncy spirited woman introduced herself as Sue and invited me to take my time looking around the store. I was surrounded and comforted at a time when my spirit had been crushed. She and I chatted during my visit about this-and-that and I told her how glad I was I missed my bus.

Sue was planning an open house for the business and she was determined to have Della Reese from *Touched By An Angel* be the special guest. Out of nowhere Sue asked, "Do you know how to contact Della Reese?"

I was stunned because Sue had no idea at that time I worked as Director of Publicity for Arista Records and there was virtually no entertainer on the planet I could not contact. When I told her what I did she just smiled, looked toward heaven and said, "Thank you."

As I paid for my purchases and got ready to leave the store, Sue asked if she could put me on her prayer list. I questioned, "You have a prayer list?"

"How could I do this," she laughed pointing to the Angels, "and not have a prayer list?"

"Yes, of course. Please do put me on your prayer list."

The years that followed brought us closer together as sisters in the Spirit. She hosted "Angel Talks" frequently at the store and we became like family. She watched me re-marry, start a business where Jerry got to build the cabinetry, get pregnant, and have the baby registered in her store. My little girl was going to be named Brooke Angel.

I am a Christian woman born, bred, buttered, jellied, and jammed in the Baptist tradition and we often had conversations about her Catholic upbringing. Jerry had just completed a five-year deaconate program and I was full of questions. Sue invited me to attend a 'talk' at a local Catholic church to attain some clarity. The 'talk' was not what Sue expected it to be and sure enough as she turned around to get a look at my face she saw the back of me instead as I headed out of the door.

It was a pleasure for me to draw Sue into my inner circle. My bestest friend Claudette and I would go by the store with lunch to just sit and talk. One day we decided to go for a "Prayer Walk" as we all agreed we were in much need of some exercise. After the walk, Sue was not ready to leave and invited us to dinner at Perkins Restaurant. We sat at Perkins for many hours into the night. When Sue called home to check-in on things she knew something was wrong when no one was home with her ailing mother. We reluctantly parted ways that night and Sue's mother parted life on earth to join our Father in Heaven. I was so glad to know that I had been with my sister friend for an afternoon-through-evening encounter filled with good company, good laughs, and good food just before one of the saddest moments in anyone's life . . . losing a parent.

When I got my Doctorate degree in Naturopathy, my teacher gave me a beautiful appreciation service where Sue eloquently and hysterically spoke of how we two unlikely ladies' lives are forever enmeshed because we are like-minded and like-spirited. I am thankful to have that event documented so that I may press 'play' anytime self-doubt tries to rear its ugly head in my life.

Now, though the miles may separate us, there is nothing that can separate us from the love of our God that we share and the love for one another.

I have indeed had a real life encounter with an Angel, and I am proud to forever call Sue my sister, and my friend.

* * *

This was happening while we went through the house and started gathering things for a huge yard sale. Mommy was a collector of all sorts of things, so I knew I had to get some help with this project. Thankfully, my cousin Louis had come and worked with me at *Calling All Angels* and also was a tremendous help preparing for the big sale. Pico was still going nuts at the clock. It was also at this time that Jerry (after being told he would make a good deacon) decided to apply to the Deaconate. I am not sure he ever expected to be accepted even for the first stage. He was.

After what seemed like twenty different tests, exams, and personality evaluations, Jerry was only a few steps away from being accepted into the rigorous five-year program through the Diocese of Scranton. Personally, I was thrilled since I was able to take the exact same courses for credit and perhaps earn a Certificate in Pastoral Studies.

It seemed like the perfect time to move into a different direction both spiritually and emotionally. Of course we prayed deeply and consulted with Milo and Jeffrey (Jerry's Angel) on more than one occasion. It was the end of July, right around what would have been Mommy's seventy-sixth birthday, when Michael called us and asked to speak with us about something very serious. As any parent knows, this is usually something that is not going to be good news.

Michael came home for the weekend and informed us that his lovely girlfriend Kristina, whom he had dated since he was sixteen, was pregnant. Of course our first thought was, please tell me you both have decided to keep the baby? Michael said, "yes". They were in college, but decided keeping the baby was the right decision. Of course we were both thrilled to be grandparents but, it still was quite the shock. When Michael said the baby was due in March, I immediately did the math and realized the baby was conceived at about the time Mommy died. My heart smiled and knew this baby was going to be a great light to this world.

We continued as planned with the sale of the house, but even though we had many close calls, we could not sell it. We were getting so frustrated so it was just after Labor Day when Jerry and I decided to take a long weekend to the Jersey Shore and clear our heads. Just before we left, the mail arrived and in it was the final acceptance letter we were waiting for from the Diocese. Jerry was on his way to becoming a deacon.

Also happening at the same time was totally unexpected. In June, our accountant for Keystone Cabinets passed away from a stroke. We were saddened but found a local accountant who began working for us. Unfortunately, the state of Pennsylvania and the IRS were looking for us for the past five years. We were unaware of this because we paid our former accountant for payroll taxes and sales taxes and he supposedly was making the payments to the correct agencies. We found out he was embezzling money from not only us, but, four other companies to feed his ever growing gambling problem. A total of over $160,000.00 was now owed to the government and we had no recourse.

The man died broke and with no malpractice insurance. We were in shock. Immediately, we took the house off the market since the last thing we needed was the IRS swooping in for the kill on the sale of the house. As soon as the real estate sign was taken down, Pico stopped barking at the clock. It hit us. Mommy was letting Pico know that is was not the right time.

Truthfully, at that point we were not sure which end was up and the thought of not having to relocate at that time was a blessing. When I finally had a chance to meet with Monsignor Esseff for spiritual direction, he must have sensed I was a wreck, but was acting like I was perfectly fine. He sure did call me out. He told me he saw a vision of me in a small boat with huge waves crashing all around me and I was feeling abandoned. He went on to say that even though the boat was tossing and turning in the water, a great light was shining on me from heaven guiding me along.

Here I thought I was handling all the "stuff" in my life with no problem and Monsignor Esseff saw right past it to the heart of pain I was enduring. What I came to realize, was the closer Jerry and I were growing in our walk with Jesus, the more we were being attacked by the enemy. This may sound strange to some folks reading this, but I know this to be a truth. This was not some coincidence that great things were happening for us at the same time as horrible things were slamming us right between the eyes. I remember a palm card I carried in the Angel store that read, *Coincidences: God's Way of Staying Anonymous.*

Monsignor warned me this was going to happen, especially because Jerry and I were now part of the Diaconate program. The better part of us I truly believe was numb. Otherwise, we certainly would have cracked under all of the pressure. I kept reminding myself, *A light from heaven is guiding us.*

Chapter Eight

The Follow Me Foundation

Sometimes in the midst of adversity, you find yourself inspired to turn around and follow another path. That is exactly what happened with the birth of the Follow Me Foundation. As people began to seek out spiritual direction from me, they felt compelled to leave some token of their appreciation. Of course I never charged a dime for any of the guidance that I gave since it freely came to me from God, so freely I share it.

However, many, many times folk were so grateful; they would leave money and tell me to donate it to my favorite charity. Jerry began to notice this more and more and thought perhaps we should start a charity. He figured we could begin to do good for others through the money that was raised. At first I thought he was nuts, then I realized he was right. We solicited the opinion and help of two very good friends of ours, Sue Walsh and Eileen Argenbright.

Sue has always been a very mystical and resourceful person. Eileen created beautiful art and music. These two women helped launch the Follow Me Foundation (FMF). After about four months of research, Sue was able to secure a good attorney who would help us to get established as a non-profit, 501c3 organization. This was completely new to Jerry and I so we were really grateful for all of the help they brought to the birth of the FMF. On December 8, 2000, we became official. Now what????

We prayed a lot and decided that the official head of the FMF would, legally, be Jesus Christ. I can assure you the attorney thought we were nuts. However, we insisted this was how it had to be or no go. So it was!

*   *   *

"The Angelic Communion of Saints"
-by-
Sue Walsh and Eileen Argenbright

Meeting Sue and Jerry Reynolds in 1998 was the beginning of a lifetime friendship. My partner Eileen and I had just moved to the Poconos. Soon I would come to realize that the picturesque area was touched by more than natural splendor but it was also touched by an Angel.

One day Eileen wanted to take an exploratory trip to the store *Calling All Angels*—of course she wanted to check it out. Eileen had been creating Angel art starting with visions of Angels in Action since 1992 even though she was not taught about these celestial creations. Eileen felt it was a good sign that this wonderful store was located nearby.

As we got closer to our destination I could see in Eileen's eyes the excitement of endless possibilities of the treasurers she might find and bring back to her art studio.

Right away Sue introduced herself as the proprietor of the shop and said, "Take your time." After a few minutes of looking around I noticed a lot of Holy stuff in the place. More than anything it was easy to see the Reynolds' were Catholic.

I told Sue that I was raised a Boston Irish-Catholic but these days I was a non-practicing one.

She said to me, "Hey, that's OK you're here for a reason, in time we'll figure it out."

Before long we became the best of friends—Jerry and I were doing a Bible study and Eileen started to work at the store. One day she announced that after much thought she was going to become a Catholic because she was deeply moved by Sue and Jerry and the many ways they lived their faith. She took Roman Catholic Instruction classes and became a Roman Catholic leaving behind the religion of her roots as a Southern Baptist. At her Holy Confirmation ceremony she took the name MaryAnn in honor of Mother Mary.

Around this time as Eileen was changing I was too. I returned to the Catholic faith of my childhood. Jerry was the kind of guy who was solid as a rock. He gave me awesome guidance with canny answers to my metaphysical questions. This entire set of changes made my mother very happy for sure!

On October 13, 1998 we found ourselves at Nancy Fowler's farm in Conyers, Georgia. She was a devout woman who had visions of Mother Mary and Jesus. The day we attended the talk on her visitations was Nancy's last public appearance. Tens of thousands of people came to the farm to hear what Nancy had to say. It Nancy's talk that day had special warnings for Catholic priests. She spoke in private with the priests of a great tribulation coming from heaven in judgment of a falling away from their vows. Didn't she hit the nail on the head with that chastisement! Soon after this disclosure, the world-wide epidemic of Priest sex scandals was made public.

Sue was deeply inspired by Nancy. "I ask you to make consecrations to the merciful, loving Heart of my Son, Jesus, and to my Immaculate Heart. Make your home and rest in our Hearts, dear children . . ." Sue really felt Nancy was speaking the truth to her soul which solidified her determination to do something honorable, productive, and inspiring in service to God.

As I look back I believe it was there at the farm a mustard seed was planted in Sue's heart. She went forward with a mission to create The Follow Me Foundation.

On July 16, 1999 like his father, JFK Jr. died young—in a plane crash. This news stunned the country and it was personally devastating to me. Growing up in Boston, I had been around the Kennedy's throughout my life. Eileen noticed how sad I had become over the awful news of this tragedy and suggested we take a ride to the Padre Pio Centre in Barto, Pennsylvania. There I spoke with Vera Calandra the founder of the Centre about my grief and we soon became close friends.

Sue and Jerry met the Calandra Family at their beautiful home that included the original Padre Pio Centre located in their barn. They spent time with Vera and Harry and enjoyed their stories of Padre Pio. Vera even invited them to a dinner to meet the Papal attaché of John Paul II. At dinner Vera explained to us all how she got to know His Holiness John Paul II. Also she invited us to go on a Papal visit with her. I believe seeing what Vera had achieved as a mother of six and a housewife of an Italian grocer, inspired Sue to want to build a center called the "Heart of Holiness".

After the visit to the Padre Pio Centre, Sue's idea of creating a non-profit organization began to grow quickly. Pretty soon more people joined in the effort and numerous activities for the community were created. Together Sue, Jerry, Eileen, and I became co-founders of the non-profit organization that Sue amply named the Follow Me Foundation.

Eileen put together the FMF Arts Institute. She donated her gifts and money plus lots of time to the Institute. Eileen created classes in "Sandscape", Art, Mandela's, and music. She also co-created music to the divinely inspired words from Sue's angelic guides. Others who came to be apart of the work of this dedicated Body of Christ were also as generous.

When America was hit with the enormous tragedy of 9/11 in 2001, Sue's reputation as the Angel Lady was widespread especially in the Pocono community. She was called upon to assist victims of 9/11 and their families in the area. This was definitely a time to be calling all Angels. Sue was at the top of the contact list for help and she went without hesitation to offer her special skills.

It was obvious the foundation needed to become a 501(c)(3) not-for-profit as soon as possible. In a short time I was able to find a good Washington DC attorney to take us on board named Bill McCambell III. Sue wanted Jesus Christ to be the head of the foundation. Bill took Sue's request seriously and placed Jesus as the head of the board of directors saying, "One thing is for sure, your non-profit should always stay above water."

Our current goal is to raise the necessary funds to purchase a tract of land in New Mexico on which to build a working organic farm and retreat center aimed at "stimulating the Spirit of God within us all."

After two heart attacks in which I had near death experiences I believe in miracles. Also, I believe in sweat equity. The power of combining these two elements with a dash of passion for what you are doing can move mountains. Amen.

*   *   *

At first, we spoke with a group of close friends and thought about what exactly our mission would be. All of us knew we wanted to be an outreach that focused on the spiritual as well as the physical needs of people. It did not take long for us to determine that a sacred place for this endeavor was needed. But as finances would have it, we needed to remain working out of *Calling All Angels*. A group of us that included Jerry, Sue Walsh, Eileen, Jo Anne, Antoinette, Josette, Jane, and I started brainstorming about how and where we could help the most people.

We thought about making sandwiches and delivering them to the homeless who lived under the Seventh Avenue Bridge in Stroudsburg. We thought about starting a soup kitchen, to feed the hungry but we finally decided to open a small food pantry to open once a month. This program was named "Food for Friends" and the people, our guests.

"Food for Friends" would be different because we did not require any proof of income or turn anyone away. I remember Antoinette saying how she ran a food pantry for St. Matthew's Church so she was a natural to lead the way. Before we even opened, Josette, Antoinette, and I were having lunch at my house trying to think of a way to ask Jerry about rearranging our office to upstairs so we could use the space for the new food pantry. We laughed because we figured if we made him think it was all his idea, he would go for it, just like in the movie *My Big Fat Greek Wedding*. Just as planned, he complied. I still crack up every time I think about it.

The first time we opened our doors, we had two people. I was crushed.

Antoinette's exact words were, "You're going to wish for these days." She was right. My heart felt only love for our "guests" as they began to frequent our service. I always felt we truly could be serving Jesus at any time, so we were always kind and loving. We opened our doors to "Food for Friends" in October 2002. It was the most humbling experience I have ever had.

I could write a book on the many experiences we encountered just within the food pantry. As predicted, we grew . . . and grew . . . and grew until finally we outgrew the little office space and began expanding into the *Calling All Angels* section of the building. Truthfully, I was ready to close the store and devote my time and effort to the FMF. It was the best decision I ever made, however bittersweet. At that point we began giving away clothing, food, which included all the staples, plus fresh produce, bread, and much more.

We had guests from all over Monroe County coming to us for help. Of course I always felt we needed to stop the grumbling of our guest's stomachs before we could talk to them about their Spirit. About a year after we opened we decided to convert the lower level of *Calling All Angels* into a chapel/prayer area. It was open to anyone who needed a sacred space to clear their heads. This also became the area in which I conducted spiritual direction. Jerry, being the talented cabinetmaker, built an awesome altar and we also purchased beautiful statues and other religious articles from a church that was closing to furnish the wonderful chapel of The Sacred Heart. We held countless Masses there, Angel Talks, Bible studies, prayer sessions as well as day retreats. It was one of the happiest times of my life. The prayer meetings involved many people from various religions.

A special core group who were Antoinette, Jo Anne, Michele, Josette and myself were devoted to helping people through deep prayer. We started a group The Intercessors, for just that purpose. The results were always astounding. When I had my Angel store, the motto was, "Expect Miracles". Here within these prayer groups were miracles happenings to many souls. God was truly working healings, conversions, and many other changes in those we prayed with. Perhaps now is a good time for some of the accounts of those people in the prayer group.

* * *

Susan Reynolds

"Angelic Prayers"
-by-
Jo Anne Tahaney

I do not remember the date or even the year for that matter. What I do remember is the over whelming feeling of peace; "Holy" is the best way to describe it.

I had heard about the "the Angel store" for a few months and finally got a chance to go there with my mother-in-law. The intention was to browse but that soon turned into much more. While perusing the beautiful Angels and religious objects, I met the proprietor Sue Reynolds. I can not tell you what we talked about specifically—but I was soon dissolved in tears. Tears of happiness and peace—all I knew was that this meeting was a life-changing event for me. God *knew* who I was and He cared about *me*—the way I always knew in my head that He knows and cares for all His creatures. For the first time I knew it in my heart—in the depths of my soul. I also knew this woman was His messenger—His instrument—His gift to a people yearning for Him. Sue and I quickly became friends.

She LOVED Jesus and exuded that Peace and Love. Don't get me wrong, she was at the same time very real, very human, with a family and friends she loved with the normal day-to-day aggravations we all have.

Sue had very special gifts. She could talk with Milo and our Angels as well. Sue NEVER wanted to be the center of attention, rather she kept redirecting everything to Our Savior, to His Love for us, and His boundless Mercy.

I remember the night we were all gathered for prayer, Sue, Jerry, Antoinette, Father Tom, and others. It was on this night—that the mission of the "Heart of Holiness" and the Follow Me Foundation was given to Sue and Jerry. Sue eventually gave up her business to make room to feed the hungry. Talk about walking the walk!

One evening, after an Angel Talk, Sue was praying over each individual—even though I was deeply engrossed in prayer, I felt compelled to open my eyes. Sue had her hands on a woman's head. Suddenly, I saw Jesus as the Sacred Heart move from "behind" Sue into her, and Sue was no longer there. This was significant on more than one level: First, at that moment I understood what Sue always said—Jesus worked through her and that it was His hands, and His healing power.

Second, and I cannot tell you HOW I knew this, but I KNEW my role was to pray for Sue as she prayed for others. And pray for others she did.

People came to Sue who were Catholic, Non-Catholic, Christians, and even Muslims, to seek guidance and reassurance, some just out of curiosity, and some just downright skeptical. The result was always the same. Not all wanted to hear the truth and some in fact turned a deaf ear but they went away knowing, they had an encounter with their Creator. As bizarre as this may sound, the evil one would try to challenge her through people who came into the store. Sue once told me of a gentleman who came in wanting to "talk" with her.

She instantly knew the challenge she was about to face and led the man downstairs to our Chapel. While I did not witness the actual encounter, Sue told him she was not afraid of him. While he seemed to become increasingly angry, by the power of the Holy Spirit she stood firm and he left. To my knowledge he never returned in the form of that particular individual. Throughout her ministry the evil one continued to harass and threaten her—verbally and even physically.

Sue was and is firm in her Catholic faith and was never afraid to uphold the teachings of Holy Mother Church. She was not uncomfortable upholding Church teaching on difficult or "unpopular" subjects. She reaffirmed the power of the Sacraments and the Magisterium of the Church while respecting the faith of others. She was not one to "sugar-coat" the truth in order to "get along" with others. She reinforced God's love for ALL His creatures. She also reminded us of how sin hurts our Jesus . . . and she did at times weep bitterly over His pain.

I suffer from migraine headaches. While staying with Sue and Jerry in Wellsboro, Pennsylvania I felt a horrible headache start to come on. I asked Sue to please pray over me. She put her hands on my head and gently pushed downward. She started to pray in another language with force, and with, I can say, mercy. As she did this, my eyes were closed and I could see myself under green water I knew it to be salt water. Somehow I was able to see a hand of a man on my head and I KNEW it was the hand of Jesus. After she finished praying she explained to me that Jesus had baptized me in the Jordan. He was making all things new. I still have migraines, but that moment brought me to healing that right now only He knows. You NEVER walk away from an encounter with the Almighty unchanged.

I remember when the tone of Sue's prayer changed. She had always been able to speak with Milo—but at some point what she was "hearing" did not fit what she knew in her heart to be true. Knowing that the evil one can take on anyone's voice, she pleaded with Jesus to silence the voice of her beloved Milo—and to be able to hear only HIM—since the evil one could not ever imitate the voice of God. The days of this prayer for Sue were not easy. She suffered both physically and spiritually. The Good Lord answered her prayer and she no longer heard Milo's voice.

I remember feeling very sad as I grew to love Milo and interacting with him. Sue assured me he was still with her and would playfully tug at her chin to let her know he was there. Now when Sue prayed over us there was a point that her tone changed. She spoke what I knew in my heart was ancient Arabic (again do not know why I am so sure, but I am). You knew that Jesus was expelling demons, that He was healing, that He was claiming His people for Himself, and He again was procuring our salvation.

When we gathered for prayer Sue would name the Saints gathered with us, the Angels, and even our Most Blessed Mother. When Jesus presented Himself, she told us that all the others faded to the background, while the Angels continued their songs of praise. When our deceased loved ones gathered with us, she would tell us what they needed us to know. For on one occasion it was my Mom telling me what only I knew, things I had never even said to her while she was on the this earth but felt in my heart. True moments of healing . . . . If you would ask Sue to recount the messages she could not, as they were meant only for us, when the messages came from Jesus or His Mother.

When my father passed into the arms of Our Lord, Sue was there to help him and me. She watched him hold my face and comfort my sister Kerri. She saw Our Lady and Her Son as the Divine Mercy (an image that depicts Jesus with rays of white and red flowing from His heart) come to be with him and safely take him home.

I watched many lives be transformed from despair to hope; from feeling abandoned to KNOWING they were loved. Knowing that God the Father was real, REAL.

Sue taught me that love meant sacrifice without complaint and with joy. She once confided in me that while she did not enjoy the pain or the suffering, she would never give it up. Even if it meant she could not commune with her Lord, her love, and to share in His suffering. I think for the first time I understood the term "agony and the ecstasy".

Sue walks the walk and does not just talk. She gave up much—willingly. She suffers much—willingly. She is not politically correct but truthful and diligent in upholding the teachings of Jesus Christ. Through the gift of her I have come to fully understand the value of each life and of the sanctity of life. I also know that we are to LOVE all people. *WE judge not lest we be judged.* As she has said on more than one occasion, our job is love all—period. Not the sin but the person.

Sue spent time with our Lord for His purpose on many planes—in the desert, at His Passion/crucifixion, at the gates of hell and the gates of Heaven. Throughout history when the world has been in chaos and when man is at his worst because the soul is most threatened, Jesus is merciful to us by sending us messengers to call us back—to remind us He is real and to uplift us. There are many such messengers in this world today. Make no mistake, Susan Reynolds is one of them.

* * *

"The Angelic Shawl"
-by-
Antoinette Fitzgerald

As a child I drove my mother insane every time she took me shopping. We lived in Manhattan and my mother went shopping in the Bowery where we encountered many homeless people. I refused to walk any further until she gave each person money so they could buy food. Little did I know this was a preparation for what was to come into my life more than fifty-five years later to be exact.

When my husband Tim retired, we moved to Pennsylvania. I did not know a soul and was very lonely. That all changed very quickly. I went to the parish rectory for a Mass card and walked out in charge of St. Matthew's food pantry. Ronnie Baxter, the secretary, knew I was new to the community and decided that I would be good at running the pantry. I did so for more than three years. During that time, I saw Sue Reynolds serving as a Eucharistic Minister and was suddenly drawn to her. The Holy Spirit kept urging me to introduce myself, which I did that very day and nothing has ever been the same.

Sue introduced me to The Follow Me Foundation, Angel Talks, and many people who are now very close friends. Suddenly, I was no longer lonely. God had filled my life with many blessings. As time passed, I became part of the FMF prayer team. After the Angel Talks, the prayer team would assist Sue with praying over people and I was amazed at what would happen. As someone was being prayed over, God would reveal to me the message He had for that person, something that seemed completely foreign to me.

These special moments also taught me that I could and should pray with others on my own. Praying with others was essential for a spirit-filled life. The next thing I knew, the FMF was involved with its own food pantry, "Food for Friends", which was something I loved doing and I was so grateful to be involved. To me there was nothing more important than taking care of the needy. "Food for Friends" did more than feed the stomachs of the hungry; we also tried to feed the spirits. The pantry gave to everyone who came to our door, no one was ever turned away and we gave away everything God gave us—food, money, clothing, bedding.

At this time I would like to talk about my wonderful husband Tim. If it weren't for him, I could not have been as involved, since I relied heavily on him for help and encouragement. He volunteered at the pantry in countless ways and offered his help and support in every way. We only had one fundraiser, an annual golf tournament, which was a tremendous undertaking for one person, but Tim did it each year with a glad heart. He even did things he absolutely hated to do if it meant having a successful tournament. Before our last tournament, we knew the pantry was closing because we no longer had a home for it. However, it did not matter, Tim worked just as long and hard to make it the most successful one ever, and it certainly was. Thank you Tim.

In 2008, Sue and Jerry went to the Holy Land and were able to enter the Holy Tomb of Jesus and shared this experience with me. While there, they touched a prayer shawl they purchased to the stone slab where Jesus was laid and something awesome happened, the essence of Jesus was left on the shawl and on every other object like a prayer cloth or rosary that it touched.

Sue gave a shawl to me and two other women during a weekend retreat we spent together at her home in Wellsboro, PA. This has been and continues to be one of the most wonderful and precious gifts I have ever received, other than receiving Jesus in the Eucharist. God very clearly reminded me that this was not a gift just for me, but was to be shared. The Holy Spirit always leads me to those He wants me to share this gift with. When I pray, I do so with the shawl in hand or around my shoulders and I believe it makes my prayer more effective and more powerful. This shawl has blessed many people in many different ways. For some, it has brought emotional, spiritual, and sometimes physical healing. For others a relief from sadness and anxiety, but for all it has always been a source of peace and comfort and gives a sense of Jesus' presence.

The FMF, which is not ours but founded by Jesus Christ for the works He chooses, has truly changed my life. I will always be grateful to Sue for inviting me to be a part of it. It has brought me an acute awareness of the great need in the world, not only for temporal needs but especially spiritual needs. It has also taught me that where there is hunger, you must first feed the stomach before attempting to feed the mind or the spirit. The FMF, its mission, and all it represents have been a great blessing to my family and me.

*   *   *

"An Angel Just For Me"
-by-
Michele Del Monte

I have known Susan Reynolds for a great number of years and ever since God gave me her as a gift, I have come to know HIM in ways I never thought possible. My journey started when I began volunteering at the food pantry. While we shared many personal moments, one that sticks with me is the day Sue said, "We are not here to help these people (the hungry), but that they are here to help us".

In my very Italian attitude I said, "Right, they are here for me?" As time went by God showed me what Sue meant. God showed me how blessed I am and all the many gifts He has given me. My favorite gift is the gift of peace.

Sue also told me to always be myself. That one shook me up, because you see, I thought I was getting away with hiding like I had been for more years than I can count. What she allowed me to be was myself, my gay self. At first, I was scared like so many times before in my life. Scared as time went on that people there would not want to be around a gay person because, we all know how easy it is to catch, gayness!

Since then, I have learned to like myself and sometimes love myself because God doesn't make junk. I have found a God that is hard to believe sometimes, because of how unbelievably good He is to me. I try so hard to be the person He has created me to be. I am not very successful most of the time, but it is a gift to know that He is always there with an outstretched hand, waiting to grab me, and boy do I grab onto Him.

* * *

"Angelic Dreams"
-by-
Kathy "Sas" Keller

It was Mother's Day ~ May 14, 2000. I went to Sunday morning Mass alone, as my husband Tom stayed home with my two sons, Matt aged five and Ryan, six months.

Upon pulling in the driveway my sister and brother-in-law were there and saying, "Something has happened to JB's Mom and we are leaving for Philly!"

"OK, let me know what I can do for you," I said. So I drive to my house and pull in back and my son Matt yells out the window, "Dad's brother is dead!"

I entered the house and Tom says, "They found Dick in the bathroom, I have to leave for my Grandma's farm now!"

"OK, GO!" On this day, Dick, at age twenty-seven died from chemical poisoning from working on a farm. JB's Mom, in Philly had a brain aneurysm that took her life the following day. From there on our lives were never be the same.

The week that followed brought Tom's mother, his three sisters and their children from Florida. I met his brother Dick only once and he was very shy and quiet. I had two dreams of him that week; both times he was in my garage, dressed in jeans and a dark solid blue t-shirt. In the first dream, Dick was standing clothed in sunshine pouring in from the back screen door reciting some kind of religious sayings like in Hebrew or some "old language".

I did not understand a word of it, but knew it was religious or of a Godlike origin. Tom was with me but never saw him because he was tinkering with something else.

In the second dream, we are again in the garage with our bed pushed—up against the doors. My niece's friends are sitting and talking with me on the bed and Tom is to my left. There is a small staircase with a landing that leads to our kitchen door. As I look up, I see Dick standing there in his jeans and a dark blue t-shirt. I do not think he is saying anything, and again Tom did not see him.

I told no one of these dreams because I did not know what they meant or that you could be "visited" in a dream by someone who passed. So, never did I realize until later, the coincidence that all of Dick's belongings or "worldly possessions" were being kept in our garage at that time. Tom had brought all of his things back from his farmhouse bedroom to sort through with his mom and sisters. His bags of clothes smelled so strongly of pesticides they had to be taken to the barn. After the funeral service his family came back to our house and told stories, and reminisced about their lost son and brother.

Tom's mom said how her sneakers smelled from the cow barns and she put them outside the kitchen door on the landing. Needless to say that is the night I had the dream of Dick standing there . . . probably right in his mother's shoes!

The next morning I ran out to get breakfast food and upon return saw that Dick's banjo was opened up in the garage. When I asked if someone had been going through his stuff, their mom said, "Yes I did, why?"

I said, "Oh I was just freaked out a little because I had a dream of him last night and he was in the garage."

I proceeded to tell of the dreams and what he was wearing when the youngest sister Heidi says, "Oh, did you know those were the clothes Dick was found in?" Actually the dark blue t-shirt was rolled up in a ball and thrown in the corner, something that he and Heidi always did. I had no idea!

Over the next few months odd things began to happen; light bulbs would blow out quite frequently (which after a while we would say, "Come on, Dick you're costing us!"), the phone would ring and no one was there, Ryan would laugh and giggle at nothing, and I would get strong smells of perfume or cigarettes (JB's mom?) while

I was alone. But the topper was when I was in the basement one morning doing laundry, I leaned to throw stuff into the dryer and felt something hit or touch my leg. I figured it was the dog, but when I turned around there was no dog ~ nothing was there!

I said aloud, "OK, Dick don't be scaring me now!" I started thinking what is he or someone trying to tell me?

I had heard my nieces talking about three of their girlfriends who had went and sat down to talk with this "Angel Lady" in Stroudsburg. She could tell you all kinds of things about yourself and some of it about those who crossed over to the other side. She did not charge anything and was not a fortuneteller or anything like that. She was just the Angel Lady named Sue. After the last incident I thought, *OK what could it possibly hurt? I'll look her up and call her.*

A few days later I called the store. Sue answered the phone pleasantly and I said that I heard she sat down with people to talk about "spiritual stuff" and could I make an appointment?

She said, "I'm sorry but my appointment book is filled for the rest of the year and I do not have a new calendar yet to start making appointments for 2001."

She asked, "Why, what's going on?"

I proceeded to speak of the two deaths that spring and the two dreams and the odd "goings-on" since then. But it was the tap in the basement that really got my neck hairs up! I said that my husband has taken this very hard and has not been able to shed a tear for his brother.

I asked, "Is Dick trying to tell me something or get a message to Tom?"

Sue's response was, "I don't feel like your brother-in-law is trying to get a message through." She asked if he was a tease or a practical joker.

I said that I did not know him very well and I had only met him once but he was very shy and quiet. I would have to ask Tom.

She felt as though this is what it was and that he was just showing he was around. At that point she heard my baby Ryan in the background of the phone as he was playing in his Exer-Saucer.

Sue said, "I hear a baby there, is he/she yours and does he often giggle or laugh at nothing?"

I said, "YES!"

She said, "He has lots of Angels around him and Dick may come and visit him too. You know that babies can see them because they are still innocent. They have not been changed or conditioned by society of what they should see or feel."

I thought, *OK that is awesome!*

Next, Sue says, "Can I ask you a question? Are you religious? Do you believe in God?"

I answered, "Yes I am a Catholic."

When asked if I attend church I said, "I had not gone consistently but I have had an overwhelming urge to start going back to Sunday Mass ever since January 2000.

She asked, "Do you believe that Jesus is actually present in the Blessed Eucharist?"

I hesitated and then said, "YES, I do believe that the consecrated host is actually Jesus!"

She said, "OK, good!"

We chatted a little more until she said, "I feel that you will be a completely different person when you are forty."

"I'm thirty-four WHAT does that mean?"

"It is not bad, I just feel you will change or be different in some way by then, she said."

I am thinking the worst at this point—*I'm dead. I will get cancer. Oh geez what can it possibly be?* My head was spinning by this time.

Our call ended, I think with her telling me, "Just stay open, like you are. That is why you are sensing or feeling all this stuff. You are being open-minded to it."

I asked if I could call her later in the year or in the New Year to make an appointment to talk. She said sure!

Years later she told me, "You know that day you called, well I used to get a lot of strange and weird phone calls from people, but God stopped me and said, *"Listen to this one! Because from here will start a very special friendship!"*

The months went on, the holidays passed and I lost my Father on January 8, 2001 to Alzheimer's disease at the age of eighty-four. It was a life-changing event even though I knew it was for the best and even prayed for it. We still would have lights flicker, bulbs pop, and phones ring; we laughed and said, "Hi Pop. Hi Dick!"

But on the morning of February13th, I looked around my house and thought, *I don't have a Cross in my downstairs. If someone came in they wouldn't know I was Catholic.*

I have them in our bedrooms, but I needed one for above my entrance door. So I bundled up my fifteen-month-old son Ryan and said, "Let's go, we are taking a ride to town to *Calling All Angels* to buy a cross!"

I arrived at the store wondering where this Sue Reynolds I had spoken to months before was. I introduced myself as the one who had called months earlier about the brother-in-law. She was very hurried, as she said she had to be in Scranton soon. She kept apologizing as she is walking quickly throughout the store, gathering her things but talking to me and telling me "stuff" that I would never forget.

I said, "No, go ahead, I didn't mean to bother you." I see this rustic silver Crucifix hanging on a wall and asked how much? She takes it down, but there is no price on it and it is the only one in the store.

She says, "Hmmm, how does ten bucks sound?"

I say, "Great I'll take it. Thank you!"

She continues to hustle and bustle around and tells me, "The Angels will write a word on your heart for the next thirty days."

"HUH? What do you mean? How will I know the word? I don't understand?"

She repeats, "The Angels said, 'Pray as hard as you can for thirty days! Praise the Lord and give Thanksgiving. Use no specific prayer, just ask that you may be filled with the Holy Spirit, (in order to receive the gift of awareness)."

She continued, "You are the one that is open and aware. Your father is around you and your son and your family needs help to get through the grieving process. You are being chosen to help them through it. God and the Angels want you to pray for the Holy Spirit for the gift of understanding.

Sue went on about my mom, siblings, and their grieving, and then says, "Your father has a very distinctive voice? Does he?"

"I guess so?" I said.

"Well to me he does!" At this point I am thinking, *Wow she hears His voice?*

The next thing she says is, "I see wood and hands. Was your dad a woodworker or had a hobby on the side?"

"Not really, he was boxer. He used his hands at that, and he was a Merchant Marine."

She says, "Oh sorry, he is around the one who works with wood or around wood. Ummm, he's with the one who works with wood with his hands!"

I said "Who, Jimmy?" Tears filled my eyes. I say in my head, *He's with Jimmy? I didn't know you were with Jimmy!* What a feeling I got inside. Unexplainable!

Sue continued, "Your Dad is with the one with the wood and around him because he is hurting and in a lot of pain. He is trying to comfort him a lot, but can't get through."

At this point I am really freaked out! Sue is still saying how she must go and is sorry to rush me and can't talk.

I say, "Go, I am sorry and I didn't mean to keep you!"

She says let the Angels give you the words on your heart and call me in a month and we will talk more.

I said, "OK, I will and thank you so very much!" I left that day with my new cross, my baby in my arms, and my mind and soul in a whirlwind. I could not wait to get home to call my sister Rita. She would never believe this!

And so it began . . . For the next thirty days I am not sure how or why I heard these, but I did:

Messenger, strength, support, love, family, soul, Mom, joy, cleanse, doves/peace, Ten Commandments, prayer, kids, aware, guidance, friend/neighbor, home, recognize, life everlasting, hope, nature, The Light, faith, Word, sister, patience, channel, death, gift, and courage.

**** "Angels words are filled with "Light, joy, peace, wisdom, love, courage and confidence . . . ." That comes from GOD. ****

I got five out of seven of them!!!!! As I am just finishing up this chapter at midnight, something very profound just struck me! As I typed all the words and dates, I noticed it ended with the date of March 14th, my fortieth birthday.

On July 13, 2005 I was told I was pregnant. I was in disbelief because my oldest was almost eleven and my youngest nearing six. I was done having babies. But lo and behold our daughter Sarah Elizabeth was born . . . . yep you got it, on my fortieth birthday. Oh Lord, you are so funny!! Thank you JESUS!

*   *   *

It was in June of 2002 that Jerry and I went on our first pilgrimage with Father John Campoli, Mary Buckman, and a great group of pilgrims to the canonization of Padre Pio in Rome. Being at the Vatican and attending the canonization with Pope John Paul II was such an amazing spiritual event, to say the least, it was a life changing experience.

We traveled to Assisi for a couple of days and it was there that I fell in love with the Franciscan Way of St. Francis of Assisi. He embraced the teachings of Sacred Scripture, and Sacred Tradition, with a Spirit of Christian humanism that relates to all learning about Jesus Christ. He encouraged being empowered by the Holy Spirit to follow Jesus Christ more closely and being totally consecrated to God whom we strive to love above everything else by living the gospel and sharing the gospel in a personal way. Because having concern for the poor, care of creation, and peacemaking are just as important today as they were 800 years ago.

Something changed drastically in my heart and mind when I walked where St. Francis walked and studied his amazing life. This was a way of life I knew I wanted to incorporate into my own. There were so many "miracles" that we experienced on this pilgrimage I could fill a book.

What I can say was my soul, mind, and outlook on just about everything changed because of this special time. When we returned, I knew I wanted to become a Secular Franciscan. This time also brought about a clearer mission for the FMF.

Somehow The Holy Spirit revealed His plan. While at *Calling All Angels*, just before we decided to close the store, a friend of mine, Laura Melber and I were having a wonderful conversation as always, when a vision came to me. I saw a great plan for the FMF. It involved a "safe haven" as it was shown to me, called The Heart of Holiness.

There was a beautiful area with organic vegetables growing and people from all religions as well as ethnic backgrounds walking up a slight hill towards the front door of this Holy place. There seemed to be many people moving about doing work and also praying. At first I wondered what the purpose of this place was, then I was told. This place would serve as God's gas station, so to speak—a place where people could be filled-up with God's loving presence and then be able to go back into their lives and share this amazing feeling with others.

We would be self-sufficient and protected by what looked like a multitude of Angels above us facing toward heaven in a dome like manner. During the vision I could see people smiling and working together side-by-side. On a train from Venice, Italy to Assisi, I was told we could have a bakery to provide four types of artisan breads to be sold at the location as well as via the Internet.

A fifth type of bread would be available seasonally. This bakery would be called, *Pane Della Pace*. That is Italian for Bread of Peace. I had no idea what all of this meant. Still, I knew it was real. What was so interesting about this vision was that Laura is a psychologist and could have easily thought I was totally nuts.

However, she was as amazed as I was that this information was being given to me. The question remained, *What are we to do with this*? Little by little more thoughts emerged from this one vision. We began looking for land so we could build a retreat house with all of the components that first appeared in the vision.

Now I felt as though this mission was a top priority all the while nurturing the various programs we started. The FMF consumed my every thought. All I wanted was to accomplish whatever the Lord entrusted to us with dignity and respect for all people. All honor is supposed to go to God. For the most part, that was always at the forefront of every project and person we encountered. However, sometimes as I well know, the ego gets in the way of what God is really calling us to do.

The board members were always supportive of the vision becoming a reality. At times I know I got carried away with what I thought God was asking of us and what the truth was. The truth was and always has been to love every person with a love that was not forced or conditional but true and Christ-like.

Let's take that one step further, each person we encounter, including ourselves, has Jesus' DNA within them. Therefore we are not just a reflection of Him but we are Him. We are the living, breathing, loving Jesus. If not, then who are we? Everything inside me wants to cooperate with the Holy Spirit that breathes life into me each and every moment but of course the human frailty we all possess somehow manages to squash that deep yearning, that divine voice which longs to be heard and seen by the world.

At that point in my walk with God, I knew I had to heed to the teachings of St. Paul when he spoke of dying to oneself and living for Jesus. The way I figure it, if I am going to be a fool, even thought of as foolish, I was going to do it for Jesus. Again, a major shift in my life was happening.

*   *   *

"The Angelic Pilgrimage"
-by-
Beulah Buzzi

In March of 2003, a female friend invited my husband and I to meet friends of hers who were visiting Milan, Italy for the first time. We had pizza together and then walked these new acquaintances to where they were staying at a convent. This brief encounter with Susan who was led to pray for me intensely that night, was to be the beginning of an important change in my life.

As a child growing up in Jamaica, there was no escape from attending Sunday school where moral lessons were taught from the Holy Bible and verses repeated and memorized to reinforce better understanding.

As I matured into adulthood and the harsh experiences of life seeped through my veins, I often recall the teachings of those who in the end, betrayed our trust. As a result of such betrayals my faith slowly dwindled away. This dwindling of faith culminated when my mother passed away at the early age of sixty-five just at the time when I was in a position to offer her a better life. While losing my faith in the God that created me, I created a tremendous void that made me very unhappy.

Establishing a Children's Home in memory of my dear mother did not seem to fill that void and immediately following the inauguration of this home, I was diagnosed with breast cancer. Consequently I had to face massive chemotherapy and a bone-marrow transplant. Added to this physical and emotional trauma there were endless problems with my son who was unable to find his path in life and a husband who expected perfection at all times. I was anxious for some positive changes and eager to fill that void but could not find the true answer. Trauma was added to trauma until I met Susan.

The long distance contact with Susan gradually drew me closer to believing in prayer once again. Not only did Susan pray with me, she and Jerry also visited me at the Children's Home in Jamaica. Her ministering to both myself and the children has left a lasting effect on us and we treasure the time spent together.

The spiritual connection that links me to Susan is difficult to describe. I seem to always know when she is praying for me and I am fully aware of a divine intervention whenever she does. Her revelations are also startling and I am convinced that God has blessed her to be a blessing to others in a very special way.

*   *   *

Chapter Nine

A Special Connection Indeed

It was about this time that various people were really beginning to become a major part of my life and the life of the FMF. One such family was The Gentile's. I had come to know the Gentile's through Josette Warfel. She and Janice Gentile are sisters. The first time I actually met Josette she had come to *Calling All Angels* looking for the Angel Lady. I remember the natural concern for her sister who had given birth to a baby boy who had severe Downs Syndrome as well as a multitude of medical problems.

I truly felt this child would be a great blessing to this family and would live. Six months later I had the pleasure of meeting the Gentile's, Janice, Fran, and baby Frankie for the first time. Immediately I formed a bond with Frankie that lasts till today. Frankie's Angel was able to communicate through Milo to me. It was one of the most amazing spiritual experiences I have ever had happen. I knew Frankie was such a gift to everyone with whom he came in contact. The Gentile's and I became instant friends and remain close. It is here I feel Janice should tell her story.

* * *

"Welcoming the Angel Baby"
-by-
Janice Gentile

My fifth child had just been born. "It's a boy!" said the doctor. My husband Fran was watching as they cleaned him up. The doctor had a very concerned look. They worked on him for what seemed like forever, wrapped him up to let us hold him for just a minute, said they needed to get him to the NICU, and they took him away. He looked OK but I kept looking at my husband like, *What's going on?*

He said, "He did not cry right away Janice. The nurses were really frantic."

No one was saying anything to us. The nurses came in with my OB/GYN doctor and one nurse taking my hand. I thought, *This is weird.*

The doctor said they think he might have Downs Syndrome. He has some of the markers that are common, but it is not definite. He was having some problems breathing but he should be fine. We looked at each other and we both started to cry.

I must admit I was scared when I received the diagnosis that my son had Downs Syndrome. *How could I handle all of this with four other kids at home. He was going to need so much help*, I thought. For just a second I asked the question—"Why me? Don't I have enough on my plate?" My husband Fran was strong. You could tell he was pretty shaken but he kept saying the baby will be fine and maybe they are mistaken.

When I told my sister, not a second passed and she said, "Oh Jan I'm sorry but everything will be fine. I can picture dad in heaven with Jesus. Jesus has the beautiful child and my Dad is saying send him to my daughter Janice she will love and guide this child. She can handle this challenge. Jan you were chosen you might not see it at this moment but you were chosen for some reason."

After she said that I felt better, I really did.

I looked at my husband, "You're right we can do this."

Everything was going to be OK. Was the world ahead of us scary? Yes. Was I still really, really sad? Yes. Maybe Fran was right. Maybe there is a reason why this little boy was sent to us. We finally got to hold him and really look at him. He was beautiful. He looked a lot like my oldest son Dominic when he was born. But I knew they were right he definitely had Downs Syndrome. I did not need to wait for any genetic testing, I could tell.

The life we thought we had planned had just been drastically altered. Immediately thoughts of what life would be like go through your head. People staring at him, where will he go to school? I kept thinking he is going to have such a hard life.

Fran called his mom and told her the news, "Mom, he has Downs Syndrome. Like that Corky kid on the show *Life Goes On*".

I thought, *Oh boy and so it begins, that's who Frankie has become our own little "Corky" the famous actor who has Downs Syndrome.*

I remember my doctor coming in to say, "Downs Syndrome kids are great, really it's not a big deal. As long as there are no heart issues you have nothing to worry about."

Well we found out we had to start to worry. After a few hours they told us the whole story. Frankie was born with four of the markers for Downs Syndrome for sure. He was born with three holes in his heart. I wish my OB/GYN Doctor was there at that moment inserting his foot into his mouth, 'Kids with Downs Syndrome are great as long as there were no heart issues.'

We got to hold him again but only for a moment. They did not let us hold him for long before he was put under a hood for oxygen because he was not doing very well. In the NICU he looked like a giant next to all those preemies. He also had pulmonary hypertension. He was big, but so sick and helpless. I was not allowed to even touch him at first because exciting him would cause him too much distress. I wanted people to say congratulations to me but no one did.

I got it. Nobody knows what to say. They feel sorry for you but at the same time they are glad it was not them. I wanted to get home, bring Frankie to meet his siblings, and get back to normal. Frankie was really struggling and they told me I could go home but Frankie had to stay. There is nothing harder than to leave a sick child in the hospital and you go home.

I had only been home a few hours when my older sister Josette called me about a wild experience she had. She lived in the Stroudsburg area and while she was getting her hair cut told her hairdresser about me, and how my life had been so crazy before but it really had been turned upside down three days ago. You see, when Frankie was born I had a five-year-old son and triplets that just turned two. Life was crazy and now just giving birth to a child with so many issues beyond Downs Syndrome, my family was a little concerned about me.

The hairdresser told her that she should go see the "Angel Lady". Josette lived in the area for twenty years and had never heard of the Angel Lady who owned a religious shop and could tell people things but she went right there as soon as she was done. Josette asked if she could talk to the Angel Lady.

The woman said, "I am Sue, but I am very busy right now perhaps you could make an appointment or come back another time."

Josette said of course and continued to browse the store. A few minutes later Josette was about to leave and Sue came up to her and simply said to her, "The baby was sent by God." She told her he was brought to my family for so many reasons one in particular was to heal broken relationships. Sue went on to tell her what a special child Frankie is and that she would like to meet him. Then she began to mention things to Josette about her own kids. They talked for a little while and Josette went home quickly and called me.

I was sitting at the kitchen table listening to Josette's story half rolling my eyes. Thinking, *Great, what is she dragging me into now.* I remember her saying, "Jan, this woman said Frankie is special."

"Yeah I know kids with Downs Syndrome are special. I'm special he's special, and only special people get special kids. I heard that a ton of times already and he has only been here three days thanks for the newsflash."

Josette then said, "Jan I never told her Frankie had Downs Syndrome. She never mentioned anything about Downs Syndrome either. She said, this baby was sent by God to this family. He was sent for a reason."

OK she had my attention. You really can't blow off a stranger saying something like that. I was intrigued and told my husband and my sisters. It did give me some comfort. Frankie was just three days old when I got the call from my sister and I had no idea how that little encounter was going to change my life.

My first night home I got a call that Frankie had gotten worse and he was being transferred to the Children's Hospital of Philadelphia, CHOP. The doctor said, "Get here fast!"

I remember someone saying to me maybe he is better off if he passes. Think about the quality of his life maybe it's the best thing. I cried out, "I don't care what he has! Just let him live God. Just let him make it."

That day was one of the worst days of my life. I remember them getting ready to transport Frankie and the nurse turned to me and asked, "Do you have a picture of him yet?"

I looked at her surprised and she said, "Let's get one for you."

I realized they did not think he would survive the ride to the hospital. He was in really bad shape when he got to CHOP. Frankie got there before me. The doctors were rushing me to sign a consent form to do this procedure. They were going to try one thing and if that did not work he would need to go on some fancy machine which was his last hope of survival.

I was taking a little too long and the nurse said, "If you don't sign these papers now he WILL die."

That's all I needed to hear. I did not care about the risks just save him. I signed and she ran off. It seemed like forever before they came in to say he was stabilized for now. We were not allowed to touch him or talk to him when we were by his bedside. Any slight noise could agitate him.

They had to put him in an induced coma to try and get him better. We called a priest from the parish to come right away and baptize him just in case.

I called my brother and his wife to ask, "Chris would you be Frankie's God parents, we are baptizing him now. He might not make it." Of course they said yes. But they were not allowed to be in the room. It was just me, Fran, and Father Joe Watson with Frankie when he was baptized.

My pastor had just gotten back from Lourdes, France and he gave his secretary Bernie a bottle of Holy water from there. Father Joe was leaving the rectory to baptize Frankie when Bernie asked, "Father Meehan is it OK if I give the Holy water to Father Joe so he can baptize the baby with it?" Imagine this lady hardly knew me but she got this sense that my baby needed a miracle and water from Lourdes (where an apparition of The Virgin Mary took place in 1858) might help him.

I was thankful Father Joe had gotten there in time. When I look back on those days in CHOP, it was where our first miracle happened. We would not know it was a miracle until much later. Frankie was fighting hard to stay with us. One day my husband and I had taken a little break and when we returned to the room, on his sheets were two miraculous medals. Of course I asked where they came from because he was not allowed to have any visitors. The nurse said a priest came in to bless him. He was just here. We immediately thought it was Father Sooner, the priest who was assigned to CHOP. We could not find anyone so we checked the sign in book to see which priest it was.

No priest had signed in. *Hmm that's weird*, we thought. We asked the nurse what he looked like but we did not recognize the description. The next day Father Joe came to see him we asked if he saw Frankie and gave him the medals.

He said, "It wasn't me."

When Father Zeuner came a couple days later, we assumed it was him we thanked him for the medals. He said, "It wasn't me."

We were thinking, *Wonder who it could have been?* Frankie turned the corner very shortly after the medals appeared. Was it the medals or the Holy water from Lourdes that did it? Probably both of those and the mountains of prayers that were sent on his behalf. He was making progress and they were hopeful he was going to survive. After about two-and-half weeks Frankie recovered enough to come home.

The therapies started right away but we had to worry about his heart. He was stable but he still had those holes in his heart. The hopes were that he would do fine and we could wait until he was about two for an open heart surgery. We were not that lucky.

By the time he was four months old he was failing to thrive and the heart surgery could not be held off any longer. At four months my little baby open-heart surgery. It was another heart-wrenching period but we prayed and he came through with flying colors. Always in the back of my mind were the words my sister told me, *he was sent by God for a purpose. He is a very special child.* I called my sister and said I think I should make an appointment to see Sue.

I have to psychics before with friends to have my fortune told. I always took it light-heartedly. I assumed Sue was like a psychic but somehow I knew this was going to be different. IF it was not, then I certainly would not bring my seven month old to see her.

We were nervous but as soon as we met Sue we were at ease.

Sue told us a little bit about herself, "I am not a psychic I am not a medium. I'm just a lady who gets messages that she is supposed to share."

We asked her if we could tape what she was saying so we could remember everything. She laughed and made us promise not to go to *20/20*. She said she liked to keep a low profile. She started with a prayer and asked God to cover her and us in his white light so we are protected.

Then we just talked. So many things happened in that first meeting. It was so healing in so many ways.

She saw my mom and dad who had passed many years ago. She told me they were right there with us in the room. I told my mom I loved her one more time and she could hear me. Sue described my mom to a "tee" even down to her laugh and the use of the word queer duck! She was there, I knew it. It was so refreshing to know that it is true; our loved ones are still a part of us. She said my grandmother was there helping me get through those early crazy days with the triplets. It was so comforting to know.

When loved ones die you hope they can hear us, see us on our wedding day or know your children. You hope and wish they see that they did a really good job raising you and you turned out OK. Sue through her Angel told us that loved ones who have passed are there for all the important events in our lives. My parents, even though they died fifteen years before my children were born, were right by their side watching over them and helping us guide them. How awesome is that? It was not like going to a fortuneteller it was different. She was definitely getting answers from someone higher than herself and she was so full of insight.

While Frankie was there he was so good smiling and cooing up at the ceiling he was really being cute! Sue was done speaking to us she kneeled next to him. She said, "He can see all of the Angels in the room."

Then she looked at me and said, "He needs to be held more." Of course I thought, *Oh, great one more thing I have to do.*

She instructed, "Get him a snuggly to carry him around. He needs to be close to you."

I was thinking, *Well she's right, but how the heck does she know I don't have time to hold him a lot.*

She knew I had a weird look on my face and she said, "You're wondering how I know this."

She had talked before about Angels and how many we have. She told us at different times in our lives we have Angels for different reasons. On that day Sue said I had the most Angels present out of everyone, like twenty-seven I think.

I was bragging and my sister responded, "That just means you are more screwed up then the rest of us."

Anyway, Sue said, "Frankie's Angels are telling Milo exactly what he is thinking and saying to them."

I was so grateful because as a mom you know what you should be doing but by the time the fifth child comes along, if they are quiet you kind of leave them be. So when someone says your child is telling them he needs to be held more, you listen.

She went on to tell me that I also need to massage his legs. "His legs hurt him a lot. He is going to have trouble with his legs and back in the future so keep massaging them," Sue informed me.

She then went on to say how special kids with Downs Syndrome are, and for what they might be lacking in their intellect they far surpass us in their spirituality. They are so close to Jesus, Mary, and all the Angels.

She said, "Frankie can see the face of Jesus just like he sees you and me." Wow pretty cool right? It is so funny she said that. This one incident in particular stopped us in our tracks.

I woke up to feed Frankie and I placed him back in his crib with his head towards the window. I woke up in a panic a few hours later and ran in the room. I looked at Frankie and he was sleeping soundly but was in a different position the blanket up to his chest. He was a month old and he barely moved during the day with his low muscle tone. So thinking that he scooted around in a complete circle and covered-up himself with the blanket was a preposterous thought.

I called my husband at work and asked him to describe Frankie's position when he left. He described how he was when I last put him down. Just like I had thought. *So I was not crazy.* Someone moved this kid—they had to.

I questioned my son Dominic to see if by chance he had gotten up in the middle of the night. Not that he could have reached over the crib rail and picked up this twelve pound kid, and lay him back nicely. Anyway I was pretty freaked out by it.

Fran comes home from work and he says, "You're going to think I'm crazy, but I went to check on Frank and as I turned my head I could swear I saw your mother sitting in the corner in the glider."

I said, "OK you are crazy." Fran does not believe in all that stuff.

Anyway he described what she was wearing and believe it or not it sounded like something my mom used to wear.

He said, "It all seemed so real, she was there and then was gone."

While Sue was talking to us about Frankie, Fran decided to bring up the scenario to her. She matter-of-factly knew exactly what happened. She said, "You weren't crazy, it was your mom." Frankie stopped breathing. We just sat there silent. Could this really be true?

Sue then started asking about when he was first born. I had not mentioned to her about all the details of his first few weeks except that he was really sick.

She asked if he had moved to a different hospital.

We said yes.

She stated, "When he was in the hospital a priest came to visit him. "Yeah a few did." She said, "No a priest in the family."

"We don't have any priest in our family."

She told us that a Father Martin, who was my mother-in-law's cousin, came to visit Frankie and pray over him. She described what he looked like; just as what the nurses described as the priest who was by his bed. Father Martin died forty years ago. He had come to bring God's healing touch to Frankie that day. It was the day he started to turn the corner. Sue also mentioned Saint John Neumann was by his bedside too.

Sue kept saying, "He is a very special child, a very special child."

It was refreshing. She had given us so much information about Angels and how God works in our lives. How He is truly present in everyone's life, every day. He knows what we are going through and He knows what we need. That day my family was given a gift, a gift that changed my relationship with God and my family.

So many things have occurred since Frankie was born. I was thankful to have Sue in my life to explain exactly what was occurring. She felt a real connection to our son and like we said we felt blessed. Sue could communicate with my son without using words. He could tell her when he was in pain, when something was wrong or when something was going really good.

The first couple years of Frankie's life we were witnessing daily visitations from Jesus. At first we asked, what is happening now? But we came to be accustomed to him talking to someone we could not see.

I remember the first time we were awakened in the middle of the night with sounds of children playing coming through the monitor. It was very real. I jumped out of bed ready to yell at my four kids for going into Frankie's room. I searched the house and found everyone fast asleep.

I woke up my husband and said, "Listen to the monitor."

There are kids talking, laughing, and playing. We assumed baby monitors sometimes pick up the sounds from someone else's house, but it was in the middle of the night and we were the only house with small children in our cul de sac.

Mornings were Frankie's favorite time. Of course they were my craziest times—trying to get four kids off to school then get Frankie ready for whatever therapist was showing up that day was quite the task. When he was a baby he was always laughing and smiling at the ceilings kicking his feet having a good old time. As he got older and could sit-up I would find him smiling and making noises, babbling with his hands telling stories to someone but he was all by himself or so we thought. He was playing with someone it was obvious, and he never wanted to get out of his crib.

I remember getting so frustrated with him. I had to drive everyone to school I had a schedule to keep. "You can't be hanging out in your crib all day," I'd say.

On one of our visits to Sue I asked her about all these happenings. She knew exactly what was going on. Frankie was getting visits from Angels, but not only that but it was that Jesus himself coming to be with Frankie. Each morning Jesus would come and spend time with my son. I don't think Frankie knew how extraordinary this was he was just excited his friend came to see him each day.

Wow, how do you go about your day when you know Jesus is hanging out with your little boy? I would just say a silent, *thank you Jesus* and smile.

Frankie loved to see Sue. His disposition changed as soon as we pulled up to her store. Frankie was pretty delayed, he did not have much speech and was not walking, and let's say, he could be a real bugger at times.

When Sue prayed over him it was a beautiful sight. He would go down the stairs to where she did her praying and from the time he was little just smile up at the ceiling or stare at a corner.

Sue would say, "Mary is over there. He sees Jesus standing next to you."

After a visit one time, when Sue had shown us a picture of Jesus, Frankie got so excited. Sue gave us the pictures of Mary and Jesus to take home with Frankie. Frankie wanted these pictures in his crib with him. Each night he would point to the picture asking us to get it for him he would give the picture a bug hug and then kiss it. Sometimes he wanted it on his pillow. He talked and smiled at the picture like it was Jesus himself. It is an amazing experience to see a small child do this. I think my other kids were pretty jealous, they did not get play time with Jesus.

On one visit Sue wanted to take Frankie to Eucharistic Adoration. I was nervous because he was very noisy when he went to church. I used to say he was saving up all his talking for when he went to church. Every Sunday from the time he was very small, church was his most verbal hour.

That day we went to church to see Jesus in the Blessed Sacrament, Eucharist. As soon as we wheeled him, in he wanted to get down. I was really nervous about that, because when Frankie gets out of his wheelchair, it is on his terms when he gets back in. He fought me and was very loud so I was afraid a scene would ensue at church.

As soon as he got down he started crawling to the altar. Sue said, "Let's just watch him."

First Frankie scooted behind the altar. He started looking up making hand gestures, which definitely had a purpose. Of course I was in panic mode because all I could imagine was Frankie pulling the altar cloth down. He then did a little exploring around the altar area, finally scooted to the front of the altar and sat there. He was looking up and then kept hitting the space next to him with his hand.

He was asking the person he saw to sit down next to him. He had a big smile and kept patting the seat next to him. We assumed he was looking at his old pal Jesus so they could play. After a few moments my heart could not handle the stress so we got him back in his wheel chair and left. I remember a woman coming out to us afterwards to tell us how beautiful it was to watch Frankie up on the altar. I wonder how many people he touched in that church that day.

Frankie spent many weeks in hospitals until his was around five years old. So many times I would have to say to the doctor to check this or run a test. They of course would look at me like, no. I would fight and yell until they gave in. Then they would come back to admit, you're right, it was his lungs, or yes he does have reflux. How did you know?

Of course I could not say, "Well I have this friend who talks to Angels and Jesus told her what it was." Instead I always answered, "Call it mother's intuition," smiled and thanked God for sending his messages through Sue.

Frankie was never an easy kid. But like all of our kids he knew how to push our buttons. Sue would tell him things and he listened. I will never forget when he was about seven and she told me it's time to start potty training him.

I thought, *OK right, the kid weighs 120 pounds, he can't walk and can't talk. How is that going to happen?*

Sue talked to Frankie told him what was expected of him. She told me what to do and said within a few months he will be trained. Sure he listened and did it. Now mind you, he never tells me when he has to go. But he is on a schedule and as long as I do not forget to take him, he is dry all the time. Truthfully I probably would have never even tried it, if she did not pass on the message. So many times I think God knew what I was struggling with and would put it on Sue's heart to tell me.

I will never forget one time I was having a really extra difficult time with Frankie. He is cute as a button but gets very angry and he is very strong.

She said, "Just get very quiet, pray, and listen to what God is saying, He will help you."

I thought, *You know what I need; I need a TO DO list for this kid! Tell God to just give me a list and I will follow it.*

I said, "This trying to get quiet to listen and figure out what I am making up in my head and what God is telling me is for the birds." I of course was kidding her. But that night when Sue was praying God told her exactly what I needed to do for Frankie every night.

The next day I got an exact list of the five simple things that I could do for Frankie; Bless him every night with oil. Have all the kids bless him. Make a special ointment for his skin and so on.

I thought, *Oh wow that makes it very easy.* Isn't it funny how God listens to everything we ask? It is a shame we do not listen as well as He does.

Once we were sitting in a restaurant and of course Sue was asking about Frankie. She stopped and said, "Someone is hurting him." She then filled-up with tears and explained what she saw. "He is being dragged out of a pool. People are pulling him and yelling at him."

I said, "Sue he is refused to go to camp in the mornings. It is a real battle. It is weird because he never gave me an ounce of trouble until last week, now every day I can hardly get him out to the bus."

She said that was why. I thought he was just being stubborn and giving me a hard time. So when I got home I asked him if he liked to school.

He said, "No."

I said, "Why?" he slapped his hand.

I asked him why and when he tells a story he talks with his hands and just says jumbled sounds. He is definitely telling me a story but I have no idea what he is saying. His eyes began to fill up.

I asked, "Frankie did something happen at school?" he hit his hand again.

I asked, "Did someone hurt you?"

He said, "Yes," and then hugged me.

It broke my heart. Sue was right he was being hurt at school.

I went to camp the next day and acted like nothing happened. I inquired, "Is everything going OK? Has Frankie been in any trouble?"

The director said, "No he's fine, but he refused to go in the pool this week."

I thought this was odd because he loves to swim.

"Did anything happen last week?"

She said, "Well Frankie refused to get out of the pool. So we had to get three men to drag him out."

I said, "WHAT!!??"

She said, "He really fought them so it was very difficult and they had to practically drag him out by his arms and legs. It was very upsetting to us. The guys were yelling but Frankie wouldn't listen."

It was the exact story that Sue described. Needless to say I took my son of there and he never went back. Now when Frankie refuses to go to school I always take that extra time to find out exactly why.

If Sue had not shared that with me I would have thought Frankie was being stubborn and would have forced him to be someplace where he was not being treated correctly.

We have had many things happen during Sue's Angel Talks. One particular evening was extra special. Frankie always wanted to be front and center during these meetings. I tried to keep him out as long as possible mainly because he was so noisy. It was an Angel party and he loved every minute of it. At the same time some serious emotions were coming-up for various people, so it was not always appropriate to have a kid rolling around the floor laughing and yelling with excitement.

One particular evening Sue was praying over people and Frankie was really animated and noisy.

Sue turned to him and said, "Frankie will you pray over me?"

He responded, "Yeah."

What happened next was probably one of the most significant experiences of my life. Frankie got up in a chair and Sue knelt in from of him. He got very quiet and lowered his head. He then took his two hands and placed them on Sue's head exactly as Sue had done when she was praying over others. Frankie kept his hands over her head and was quiet for at least a minute, could have been longer.

The energy in that room was incredible. We were in awe, Jesus was working through Frankie to pray over Sue. It was evident in so many ways. You see, if you kneeled down in front of Frankie in any other circumstance two things would happen, he would grab you by the neck and bonk your head against his, or he would tickle your neck really, really hard. Frankie is never quiet and still and certainly would never gently rest your hands upon your head and sit still for any period of time. We were all given a very special gift that night.

In 2007, I discovered that I had a mercer staph infection on my lower abdomen. It started as a scratch and got infected. When the Doctor saw it, he stepped back and said, "Oh my God." The cyst that formed was quite large.

I was immediately admitted into the hospital and a surgeon was called. They first wanted to try antibiotics and talked to me about my out-of-control diabetes and how that could be a contributing factor to how bad the cyst had gotten. My doctor was really trying to scare me straight.

She said, "You have small children and this is very serious. If we do not get it under control, we will have to open this up, put a drain in it, and you will be out of commission for a long time."

I was scared and I started to beg God to let me escape this one. You know the drill—promising this and that. Was this as serious as they were saying? Could I have really died? After a few days I was discharged. I was told to do nothing but rest and hopefully the cyst would continue to decrease in size. If it did not, surgery was to be the next step. *OK sure, do nothing but rest*, I thought. Well Sue had decided she was going to come and stay with me for a few days with my sister to help me out.

Of course I have to *clean* my house before I have people come stay at my house. SO there I am vacuuming and cleaning-up instead of resting. Bad idea. I was in tremendous pain and the cyst had actually gotten worse. I got the message and went to bed.

I was having a nice visit with Sue and Josette and when we were about to head to bed. Sue asked if she could pray over me. There we were sitting in my kitchen as Sue put her hands on my head. As she is praying I am getting very warm. I start to feel warm water running down my leg. I'm thinking, *Oh my God did I just wet myself?* A very strong tingling sensation came through my body. I was extremely hot and still felt this trickle down my leg. I really thought I was going to pass out. Sue finished and I said good night not wanting to get up for fear that I did have an accident.

I stood up and my pants were dry, my socks were dry. I thought, *Now that's strange*. I went to get ready for bed and I looked down at my cyst. It had seriously shrunk in size. I am talking to the point where I thought, *Where the hell did it go?*

I went to Sue's room and said, "Oh my God, it's almost gone."

She was just as shocked as I was. We thanked God and went to bed.

Truthfully, I figured when I got up in the morning it would have gone back to being a huge cyst or at least had grown again. But it was smaller yet. Definitely almost healed.

Sue left and I continued to rest as ordered. Monday morning I went to the doctor, when they asked how I was doing I said, "Great."

When they checked the cyst he stepped back with a look, where did it go?

Not wanting to say, "Oh, I have this friend who prayed over me and it disappeared. I simply said, "I rested and prayed all weekend."

He said, "I don't care how much you prayed, no way could something that infected and that big go away in two days. "Do you know how lucky you are? These infections are very hard to get rid of. We thought we were going to have to schedule surgery on you to put a drain in."

I smiled and thanked God.

I guess I am pretty stubborn even after that scare I was good for a while, but as years went by, I left my diabetes un-attended Sue had told me about pain in my toes years ago and to watch the sugar. Then I got an email from Sue asking how I was feeling. She informed me that she was being awakened at night because of me. She had a strong feeling I needed to get checked out. Something was wrong.

OK that was my wake-up call. I called the doctor the next day and started back on my medicine diligently. My AC1 was 9.6 and my diabetes was way out of control. Thankfully I can say that my sugar level is getting back on track and I have lost thirty pounds. I can thank Sue for seriously taking the messages from God and passing them on that I was ignoring daily.

As I write these memories I am embarrassed. God has touched my life in very real ways. He has been in the presence of my son. Jesus himself, Mary herself right there in my home. How do you go back to regular life and just go about your day? But that is what I did often. My son sitting there by himself cracking-up laughing, yet no one is around. I know exactly what is happening, an Angel is playing with him or maybe Jesus Himself.

Yet, I turn around and yell at my kids to pick up their rooms. Thank God He is so forgiving. I look back at all these instances that have happened in my life, daily miracles, major miracles that I have taken for granted. I am sure I am not the only one who takes God for granted. You would think because Jesus has daily playtime with your child it should make me change something about myself. We all struggle to be the person God wants us to be.

As of this writing, Frankie is twelve years old. Sue was told when he was just seven months old he had difficulty with his legs. Today he cannot walk more than ten steps at a time, so he gets around by crawling or scooting on his butt. We continually try to get him to walk more, but he is severely overweight. He has a little speech but most of his communication is through sign language, pointing, and grunting.

One thing I know for sure is that Frankie can see things I cannot see. He knows things that I will never know. I used to feel sorry for kids with special needs, but I am starting to realize that we are the ones who we should feel sorry for they see Jesus like we cannot. They have so much to teach us if we would just take the time to see them. I also believe Frankie is a very lucky boy with a one-way ticket into heaven. How could he not, he has play dates with Jesus himself.

*   *   *

It is impossible to write about the Follow Me Foundation without including certain people's stories. Therefore it is here that I will continue to let you hear from those who were the closest to it.

*   *   *

"The Angelic Sojourn"
-by-
Nick Gemmo

A person must meet thousands of people throughout the course of a lifetime. Most of them are no more than acquaintances, a handful will become friends and even fewer yet will be lifelong friends. I am talking about the friends that no matter how long it has been since you talked to them or how many miles separate you, there is a feeling of a heartfelt connection.

I truly believe that the Lord puts people in other people's lives for a reason, whether it is for guidance, or love, or companionship, He gives us the right person at the right time in our lives. It has been my blessing that the people I have known have touched my life to make me a better person.

One such person is Susan Reynolds. I first met Sue back in 1995; she had taken over my advertising account for a local magazine in my town. I immediately took a liking to her because of her no nonsense approach to business and her confidence in what she was doing and most of all a feeling of trust. Sue also at the same time was the owner and operator of an Angel store, which was interesting to me because I have never heard of or been in an Angel store. I should have seen the writing on the wall that I was in for a ride that would change my life. I am an Italian and was baptized Roman Catholic.

I attended Catholic school until I was in the sixth grade and I went to church every Sunday with my father (most times kicking and crying). I was in my thirties when I met Sue and although I belonged to our local church, I only went on Easter and Christmas and had done so for many years. For a long time I felt emptiness in my life, that nothing could fill. As time went on and my curiosity about the Angel store grew, our friendship blossomed. She talked to me about Jesus and Angels.

I actually felt kind of stupid, calling myself a Catholic and attending Catholic school, yet knowing so little about Jesus the church itself, and the true meaning of Godly things. Slowly but surely she was opening my eyes to Jesus and what being Catholic really was.

After a period of time, my belief in God had become stronger and I was more curious. A funny thing happens to a person when they associate themselves with others, you truly become what your environment dictates. When I was growing up, my mother and father always said, pick your friends wisely. I know now what they meant. Depending upon the company you keep you will either become elevated or lowered in life. The more time I spent with Sue and Jerry I felt elevated in both mind and spirit. When a person is around someone who believes in something with all of his or her being, it is hard not to start believing yourself. Unfortunately this works with evil also (remember the Kool-Aid).

One day Sue approached and asked me if I wanted to join she and Jerry on a pilgrimage to Medjugorie, which is in Bosnia. Now,

I am up for a road trip anywhere but this seemed a little far-fetched even for me, but I asked for more information anyway. As time grew closer to the deadline date she would ask, about the trip. My response was, "still thinking about it".

That time in my life my finances were a mess and I had no one to watch my business. I was definitely not expecting to go on this pilgrimage until one fateful day.

I was sitting across from Sue at her desk. She looked at me and said, "You have to make a decision now."

Up until that point, my decision was going to be no! As she sat there and looked at me and asked again, something came over me and I said, "YES!" I did not know how I was going to pay for it, or get the time I needed, but I was going. As they say, *God works in mysterious ways,* because I found the money and was able to cover my business.

I have been on many vacations and have traveled to many far away places but this trip changed my life. The journey was incredible from the time we left the airport. My first unbelievable experience was stopping on the road where Father John held Mass on an altar carved out of a mountain. All throughout our trip I felt a feeling of serenity and peace. The place that we stayed was very simple but enjoyable and our hosts were most gracious. Each day we ventured out to find the most glorious of sites all the while praying the rosary. I probably said the rosary more time in that one week than I had in the past twenty years and I loved it. The walks we took and sites we saw, especially Cross Mountain and the 'awesome cathedral where we attended Mass, will live in my soul forever.

When I arrived back home, my friends and family could see the change in me. I was kind of surprised because although I felt different I did not think it was noticeable, until someone told me I had found my smile. That was a profound statement to me. I started thinking, *Was the unhappiness and emptiness I was feeling really that noticeable? I guess it was.* The most important thing I came back with was my smile and everything that caused me to smile . . . Jesus!

*   *   *

"The Angelic Painting"
-by-
Francine Gillen

When thinking of all the incredible experiences of faith I have had while knowing Sue Reynolds, there are two stories standing above the rest.

My most incredible experience with Sue was being given the opportunity to create a painting illustrating her vision. I have wanted to be an artist for as long as I can remember. Painting and sculpting is the one thing I find myself getting lost in and am truly passionate about. There have been a few times in my life where the work took on a life of its own and I knew it was not just my hands creating the work. Painting Sue's vision was one of these times.

I was truly in awe when I first heard the story of Saint Faustina. Jesus gave her an image and told her to have the image of the Divine Mercy of Jesus painted. I was sitting before the Blessed Sacrament (Jesus in the Eucharist) when I first opened a book on St. Faustina and learned about this painting. I cannot describe how moved I was by this story and the impact it had on me. When Sue described her vision and said Jesus told her to have this image painted, I immediately thought of the Divine Mercy image and how inspirational it is. I knew this image was coming directly from Jesus, and for some reason he chose me to do it. I felt truly blessed to serve the Lord. There was no question of whether or not I would do it, and accepting money to do this was not even a thought.

I sat at my desk on the phone talking to Sue as she detailed her vision of a Jewish man dressed in traditional clothing and a Muslim man dressed in his traditional garb. She described Jesus in the middle with his eyes lifted upward to the light of the Holy Spirit in the form of a dove, and the three figures were bathed in light.

As we talked images formed in my mind of what this painting looked like. It was not long before I began researching Jewish traditional clothing, Muslim dress, and the faces of the people of both religions. I also researched the landscape of the Middle East.

Small rough sketches were done, and then I took a sheet of brown paper, and with pencil and white conte crayon put the vision to paper. As rough as it was I sent it off to Sue and waited for her critique.

"My Peace I Give To You"

It was not long before Sue let me know that the sketch was exactly what she had envisioned and to proceed with the final painting. I began buying the materials and stretched the canvas on my living room floor. I set up my easel in the back room of my house where I get a lot of sunlight. I know in the beginning stages of the painting, things were coming together well. I was working on it here and there along with my other job teaching art at an elementary school.

Some time had passed since I began the project, probably weeks or even a month since I had started when I had saw Sue at a healing Mass.

After the Mass Sue took me aside and said, "Don't let sin get in the way of getting this painting done."

Needless to say I was very struck by this comment and asked her to elaborate but I got nothing more. I thought a lot about it and still unsure of all the comment meant I knew I needed to buckle down to get the painting finished. I needed to stop letting distractions prevent me from focusing on the task at hand. I needed to allow myself to be in a state where Jesus could work through me.

At times while painting I would hear things like, "add more light". I know that the Lord worked through me in this painting—it was not just for me.

When the painting was done I drove it to Sue. I could not have asked for a better reaction. The image was apparently exactly what Sue saw in her vision. She was very pleased with the finished piece.

I am extremely grateful and humbled, and truly hope this painting serves all who are intended to be blessed by it. What a gift to be able to use my God-given talents to serve the Lord. I truly hope that more opportunities like this are given to me.

The second most striking experience I had with Sue was in 2002. I was going through a very difficult time in my life with a divorce, raising a daughter on my own, having serious financial problems, and struggling with depression. Life was not easy at that time. This was going on for a long while and I spent a lot of time praying about my situation. I remember sitting before the Blessed Sacrament many times. I made up a little prayer that I said when I sat down in front of the Blessed Sacrament in this small chapel of my church. I said,

"Lord, please fill me with your light, fill every cell of my body with your light." At my most difficult and desperate times this prayer would be repeated in my head.

I never told anyone this prayer I said, and not sure if I had heard it somewhere or if it was just something I had made-up. On one particular morning I was really in a bad way, feeling desolate, and like things were overwhelming, I called Sue and asked if I came to have her pray over me.

I talked with Sue about all that was going on. When it came time Sue and her husband Jerry, prayed for me. At first she spoke in tongues and there was no doubt in my mind Jesus was present. As she kneeled in front of me my eyes were closed and I believe her hand was on my head.

The next words she said were, "I am filling you with My light. I am filling every cell of your body with My light."

There is no doubt in my mind that it was Jesus speaking through her, speaking directly to me letting me know in my most desperate moment that he heard my prayer and was with me. Needless to say it was a powerful healing experience.

Words cannot express what an impact Sue has had on my life. Her willingness to share her gifts has brought my faith to a higher level than what it was before I met her. She has truly been a blessing in my life, and I am truly grateful for all we have shared.

* * *

"Skeptic Meets an Angel"
-by-
Mary Ilkew

At first I was a little skeptical of Sue when I first met her but then I realized she was genuine. I noticed only good fruit produced by her efforts. I remember one time helping in the food pantry and I commented about a woman coming for food with long, polished nails.

She said, "Maybe that is all she has going for her."

It taught me a lesson about being judgmental.

When my Mom passed away I was having a very difficult time. Bo, my husband and I visited in Wellsboro for a few days. I am so grateful for her spending time with me even though I was not good company. I felt better being with her. God's love shines forth in Sue and Jerry both. I always feel welcomed and loved with them. I pray God gives them the strength and wisdom needed to carry out the work He has called them to do. I pray God blesses them abundantly.

*   *   *

"Angelic Teachings"
-by-
Louise Latzko

I was introduced to Sue in 2002 by my nephew who attended East Stroudsburg University. He contacted me shortly after Sue spoke during one of his classes on Angels. Joy and excitement overflowed in his voice about what he experienced. This left me thinking that something extraordinary must have taken place there. I felt compelled to meet Sue as soon as I could arrange it.

At her store named *Calling All Angels* I was able to meet this "Angel Lady" and I traveled an hour from my home in Dallas, Pennsylvania. As I entered the store, Angels were everywhere. I was enchanted by the serene place I had just entered—almost instantaneously, I felt very comforted and was thrilled to be there.

From the moment I was in her presence, I sensed something very special about her. I felt at peace being around her and there was an immediate connection I had never quite experienced before. When I gazed into her warm eyes, I felt as though she looked right through me into my heart and soul. It was a strange feeling but yet very comforting and reassuring in some way. We went to a private area to talk.

Little did I know that day I had met a true friend, confidant, spiritual counselor, and mentor. She shared some things she saw and sensed around me and mentioned things no one could have ever known from meeting me for the first time. Her words and spiritual wisdom left me with an inner sense that truly Angels were surrounding me and many saints were guiding my pathways. Suddenly, I realized what all of my nephew's enthusiasm was about, since I was now experiencing some of the same feelings. I now had to find out why God placed her in my life and what I needed to learn from her.

At the check-out counter was a donation box called "Food for Friends" where you could make a donation for the food pantry of the Follow Me Foundation. I asked Sue what I could give her for all the time that she so graciously spent with me, but she answered softly, "Absolutely nothing. No money is needed for doing God's work."

I felt so blessed that I not only wanted to give a donation in the box for the food pantry, but I also wanted to know more about this special "Angel Lady" and the Follow Me Foundation from the brochure. Everything in the brochure is what I felt strong about in my heart, and I knew then God must have arranged this meeting.

A few weeks later, I decided to go there again and was stunned at all that was happening. I spent the day at the foundation to observe and to help out in some way of feeding the hungry and being a part of the FMF's great work.

Many volunteers were vigorously working in different capacities. It truly inspired me—from sorting all the donated food items, to filling bags of food for pick-up, to sorting out clothes, and household items. I immediately felt a sense that this was, without a doubt, God's work. The Follow Me Foundation was a model for following what Christ told us to do and to follow Him in the many ways He calls each of us.

I continued to go to Stroudsburg periodically to help with some of the various activities and services that were constantly taking place there. The first Wednesday of each month was a big day at the food pantry. On this day, the people came from many outlying areas for items that they so desperately needed.

I was not prepared for what I was about to experience. Some of the children did not even have shoes on their feet when they entered the building, and the weather was already cold outside. It was heartwarming to see how so many people left not only with shoes but clothes, coats, books, toys, household items, and most needed food items. Most of all, they departed smiling and knowing someone truly cared about them enough to meet their basic needs. It gave me such a good feeling inside to experience all of this first hand, yet a haunting feeling overcame me knowing there was so much more to be done. I cried all the way home that day.

The FMF provided everything from emergency food and shelter, to help for single parents, faith sharing, Angel Talks, Bible studies, healing through the arts, spiritual support, and grief counseling, just to name a few. Sue was always looking forward to the next service or program that could also be added to this list. Thousands of people now depended on all the services the foundation provided. The various programs continued to increase due to greater needs and Sue was always praying for innovative ways to serve the people.

Finances were a challenge, too, as the number of people and needs so rapidly increased and funding dollars decreased. Although it seemed like a whirlwind to me, Sue presented herself as being calm and in control of whatever obstacles came before her.

One of Sue's visions was to have a place she called "The Heart of Holiness". She worked relentlessly toward obtaining a piece of farm land where there would be many people trained in different areas to provide for themselves and work for God.

Sue often said to me, "If you give the poor food today, they are still hungry tomorrow—but if you give them an opportunity to train and work for themselves, they can have the dignity and chance to provide for their own tomorrows."

The funds for such a project would come from the hearts of those who answered the call for Holiness and serving the Lord in whatever way they were inspired.

One day I had the opportunity to go to a prospective land site with Sue. As we were praying the rosary standing on this piece of farmland, we gazed upward at the clear, blue sky above, and there we all saw a magnificent, massive Angel-form looking down on us. The date was February 11, the feast of Our Lady of Lourdes. Since the sky was crystal blue, with not even one passing cloud that day, we believed this could only be a sign from God this project was something good to pursue to become a reality someday. Although that piece of land did not work out, Sue never gave up her quest to continue to find another perfect spot.

One of the many great opportunities I had was to work side-by-side with Sue was when she offered washing of the feet to the poor and homeless. It was modeled after our Lord's washing of the disciples' feet. As the guests arrived at the food pantry each month, another significant service was now available. I never felt more humbled and closest to Jesus as that first day when I took part in the actual washing of the feet with Sue.

Kneeling at the lowest part of the body with a stench that was sometimes quite overbearing, once more, one of Sue's visions was now manifested. Knowing that it was truly Jesus we were ministering to, we knelt down on the floor and took the dirt and grime off of those who said yes to the washing of their feet with soft cloths, perfumed lotions, and clean socks to top off a job was done well. Kneeling and looking up into the eyes of the one before us, you could not help but see the suffering Jesus. That moment is locked in my heart forever.

The Angel Talks Sue gave inspired all those who were lucky enough to attend. People of all faiths could connect with the concept of Angels walking along our journey with us. Her talks gathered people of all faiths, and they were a great unifier and helper of the downtrodden spirits who longed for a loving message. Sue provided us with an understanding of these heavenly messengers to light our way in a very dark world. Always uplifting in words and deeds, Sue continues these talks and works tirelessly in reaching out to others through her ministry.

The Follow Me Foundation's motto still rings loudly, as it was simply stated in that brochure I read such a long time ago, "Seek to follow God's command to share our blessings, gifts, and talents with the world as exemplified by Jesus Christ." The profound influence that Sue has in my life and spiritual journey is forever written on my heart.

*   *   *

From the year 2000 until 2009, we continued to run the FMF out of our building in Stroudsburg, PA. Thousands of people came and received help either through our "Food for Friends" program, the Blessed Baby program, or for spiritual direction. Year after year we opened the doors to what we felt God was asking us to do . . . *Take care of my children.*

However, in August 2009 Jerry and I had to sell Keystone Custom Cabinets and Woodworks after twenty-one years in business. The economy tanked and our business was on the way to bankruptcy. Jerry was aging rapidly and I was dealing with various illnesses including Common Variable Immune Deficiency (CVID), Iron Deficiency Anemia, Osteoporosis and others that were taking a huge toll on me. It was clearly time to move on.

Thankfully, we were able to sell the business, pay-off our debtors, and lease the building to new owners of Keystone. It was bittersweet. Letting go of the business after all those years was like saying good-bye to a loyal and trusted friend for the last time. We also lived in the apartment above the business so it also meant moving to our retreat home in Wellsboro, Pennsylvania.

Maintaining "Food For Friends" was not going to be easy because Wellsboro is three hours away from Stroudsburg. How were Jerry and I supposed to run the FMF from there? Initially, Jerry drove to Stroudsburg two days a week to help with the food pantry. However, the people who were now in our building did not want the food pantry run out of there. We needed to find another location and fast.

It was then a wonderful gentleman, Jim Halterman heard of our plight through one of our many incredible volunteers, and offered to let us use one of his empty buildings until it was sold. We were thankful that the new location kept the program going. It was also at this time the needs of those we served were becoming more intense as well as growing far beyond our imagination. At this point there was no way Jerry or I could continue a three hour commute plus trying to earn a living in our new city. We asked Kristina Reynolds, our daughter-in-law to take over the task of running the food pantry.

She and a volunteer named John Veit worked together tirelessly to keep things running smoothly.

It was also at this time that my health began to take a turn for the worse and eventually caused me to be unable to work. My life would never be the same. All the plans for the retreat house and everything else came to a complete standstill. If I am being truthful, it was probably the hardest thing I had to do, letting go of my intimate connection to the "Food for Friends" program. Many hours of deep prayer and contemplation left me with no concrete answers.

However, it was during this *dark night of the soul*, as they say, I came to better understand my relationship with Jesus, Mary, the Saints, and of course my beloved Angels. It was a time of pruning of the dead and out of touch thoughts and feelings that were dragging me into a place I never wanted to go to—depression and un-ending negative thoughts. I realized that my relationships with family members, friends, and especially with my God were what defined me as a person. It was not what I did in my life, but how I was able to be like Jesus to those suffering. That is what it is really all about—loving those who seem unlovable. Perhaps this is a good time to explain why I believe we are "Jesus" to others.

We have all heard the saying, "you are what you eat." As a Catholic Christian when we receive Jesus in the Eucharist, Communion, we believe we are receiving Him—Body, Blood, Soul, and Divinity, not just a symbol of Him. Therefore, we are no longer ourselves, but Jesus in the world. Of course as flawed humans, we must repent of our sins and return to the table to be fed often so we may continue to die to self and live for Jesus.

There were times in my life when I was the one unlovable and yet someone, somewhere, chose to lift me out of the ashes and love me anyway. They were all being Jesus. Each of us, as Christians are called to allow The Holy Spirit within us to ignite a flame of love, compassion, and joy for those whose path is dark. This is who I had to be. It is funny, when you are faced with a life-changing incurable disease, you either begin a new and better mindset, or you slowly destroy yourself. Oh sure, I threw myself a bunch of pity parties, especially when Jerry was out working and I was home alone talking to two Chihuahua's. But, after practically being slapped in the face by God, I knew it was not about quantity of life but quality.

God's wake up calls are never easy!

Chapter Ten

Seeking out the Sacred

Throughout my life, as most of you can relate, you encounter those who seem to appear out of nowhere, but leave an impression which lasts forever. There have been many people who easily fit that description. What continues to amaze me is, when we look back at our lives, we come to the influence of the simple acts of others. I will attempt to put a timeline on some of the "almost to good to be true" moments and the people who have flavored my journey with fragrant spices, flowers, and colors that will stay within my soul, always.

In Spring of 1997, I was told of a woman in Conyers, Georgia named Nancy Fowler who was receiving messages from The Virgin Mary. At first I did not think much of it considering the experiences I have had throughout the years, however, different people showed up at *Calling All Angels* and wanted to discuss what they were hearing about this particular Holy site. It was not until a woman whom I did not see very often, came in and said she felt compelled to let me know I was to go to Conyers for what was to be the final apparition of Mary.

Truthfully, I felt a bit confused and thought perhaps this lady was also confused. When she said it would be beneficial to bring my mother because she was in serious need of healing, I started to really pay attention. Mommy was still dealing with the affects of the heart surgery and was really in no condition to travel but, she also needed a great deal of healing. So, I let this lady talk.

When I explained my mom was unable to walk great distances, she said it was no problem because she was told to find a wheelchair to give to me. Ok, now I knew this was no coincidence. Actually, Sue, Eileen, my cousin Louie, and my Mom all thought it was a great idea to go to Georgia for this pilgrimage, the first of many. Jerry decided to stay behind and hold down the fort.

The five of us drove to Georgia in a day and a half. We stayed in a cheesy motel about half hour outside of Conyers. Who knew that just about every hotel and motel was filled to capacity? The next morning before sunrise we headed out to the farm where the visionary was located. Well, you could have knocked us over with a feather when we found out there were over 50,000 people attending, from all over the world. Other than being in church, this was the first time I had ever witnessed such an amazing gathering of the faithful.

There were rosaries being prayed everywhere, in all different languages, yet it all flowed. Trying to get to the different parts of the farm was quite the challenge for my Mom in a wheelchair. The paths were rocky, dusty and very narrow. Somehow, we did our best. At the time of the apparition, when The Virgin Mary appeared to Nancy, the entire place fell silent. The message was filled with love, hope and healing. Everyone was in awe and praying deeply. Toward the end of the day, Mommy began to have difficulty breathing and we had to call an ambulance.

The doctors in the emergency room were shocked to see the condition she was in and remarked about how lucky she was to make it to Georgia. One doctor had even gone so far to say, how many people who undergo the type of surgeries Mommy had, never make it. He said, "Mary must have really wanted to see her."

We knew something very special had happened to all of us, which could not be explained. My prayer from that point forward was to be able to visit sacred places as often as possible, rather than just for vacation. And so the pilgrimages began.

You have read about our journey to Italy, twice, but we also were privileged to go with Father Campoli to Medjugorie, Ireland, and the Holy Land. These pilgrimages opened-up my eyes to the wonder and awe of faith. As I describe them and the miracles that occurred, perhaps you too will be transported to these special places in your mind, or you may have been to these Holy sites and will recall your own events.

Medjugorie, December 2004

Medjugorie is a town located in western Bosnia, in the Herzegovina region about sixteen miles southwest of Mostar. It is here that a group of six children had reportedly seen visions of The Virgin Mary for over twenty five years. Now as adults, they receive messages and visions at various times. Again, I felt a major pull to go to this area, even though it had suffered through an awful war, I knew I would experience peace.

On this pilgrimage as well were Jerry, Antoinette and Tim, Jo Anne, Charlie, Francine, Josette, Rose, Betty, Wally, Nick, and Kathy. All of these wonderful people were connected to the FMF and were called to be a part of this experience. Once again, Jerry and I were dealing with some financial issues, so I prayed and asked God if He wanted us to be there, to help us to get the funds. At that time, Sue and Eileen were staying in my parent's house next door while their new home was being built. Sue downloaded a picture of Jim Caviezel, the actor who played Jesus in *The Passion*, and we both felt somehow this trip was connected to him.

I secretly hoped he would help us to be able to get the land for the Heart of Holiness. Sue and Eileen knew Jerry and I were struggling. At the time I thought I would not be able to go, they gifted us with a thousand dollars for allowing them to stay at our house. Jerry and I never asked or expected anything from them for utilizing our home. It was a joy to have our friends next door to us. Either way we were shocked and relieved at the same time. We were on our way as we piled into a van and headed to Newark Airport.

We were excited and scared at the same time. We met Father Campoli, Mary Buckman and the rest of the pilgrims at Newark Airport and began our long journey to this unknown little town of Medjugorje. When we arrived in Mostar, the first thing I noticed was a ton of armed guards. Everyone was a bit nervous but all I could think was, *We certainly are not in Kansas, Toto*. We were all exhausted from the flight, yet we were exhilarated at the thought of being where Our Lady, Our Mother was appearing.

Now I know to some of you are thinking we are nuts. It sounds like we were going to some celebrity event, but the truth be told, it was much more. It was our souls that seemed to long for this connection with Our Mother. We were not disappointed.

By the way, two weeks before we were ready to leave, I tore my meniscus in my knee and was in major pain. The doctor told me I might need surgery and to stay off the knee. I was on crutches and was told not to climb or put any strain on the knee. So what was the plan??? I was going anyway. I was not going to let a bum knee stop me. Yes, I knew we would be climbing up apparition hill and Cross Mountain, but I also knew that the enemy was not going to stop me from making this trip. Deep in my soul I knew a healing would take place. We would be in this Holy place during the feast of the Immaculate Conception, December 8th, which also was the date we started the FMF. This was more than synchronicity.

A few days into the trip we went to see the priest who was instrumental in helping the children. At the time of the first apparition, the children were thought to be lying. The government, which was communist at the time, wanted no part of this hocus pocus, so they made it very difficult for them. Father Jozo, a Franciscan priest was told during prayer to accept the children because they were telling the truth. After many years of torture, he was finally released back to a parish and we went to hear him speak.

We walked into what was nothing short of a church basement and began to pray. The place was packed and everyone was anxious to hear Father Jozo. After a few minutes he was introduced and began to tell his story through an interpreter. Fifteen minutes later, he told us he had a special guest who would also like to speak. This man came out and looked very familiar to me, but he started speaking in broken English so I figured I must not know him.

All of a sudden, he spun around and said, "It was a miracle, I can speak perfect English now."

I thought to myself, *what an idiot*.

He then began to talk about his conversion story. He spoke about how during the making of the film, *The Count of Monte Cristo*, he felt the presence of Jesus and The Blessed Mother and how his wife wanted him to come to Medjugorje. At that point it hit me that this actor was Jim Caviezel.

I looked at Jerry and we were both completely blown away. For whatever reason, I got up and went to the back of the room. I was shaking as I sat there alone, wondering what all this meant. However, I noticed an older man sitting way on the other side of the room alone in the back as well. He looked at me and smiled and just shook his head as if to say, 'Yes, go ahead and talk to Jim.' Who was this man?

After the talk, I raced down to Jerry and asked him if he thought I should talk to Jim and of course his answer was, "Heck yea." I asked Jerry and the others if they noticed the man in the back of the room sitting by himself. No one had seen him. Was I imagining this? Absolutely not. I know what I saw, so I assumed it must have been an Angel. When I finally spoke with Jim about the Heart of Holiness, he looked at me as though I was a little nuts. I figured I would never see or hear from him again so I gave it my best pitch.

A day later we were invited to an orphanage to pray with the children when the director told us they had a surprise for us, a special screening of *The Passion* (before it was even released) with actor Jim Caviezel. Crazy right? Jerry and I sat right next to him as we viewed the movie in a make-shift recreation room. At one point during the movie I became so upset by the gruesome scenes that I had to leave. I went to the restroom to wash my face. As I was exiting, Jim was coming out of the men's room and we nearly banged into one another. We spoke a few minutes and I told him that I felt that heaven had brought us together and now it was up to him to decide if he could help us. He took my business card from the FMF and said he would be in touch. He has never called.

One morning I was awakened by the Holy Spirit and instructed to go to the balcony facing Cross Mountain to pray. Naturally, I did. What I saw was nothing short of a miracle. Immediately I woke up Jerry. He acted like, are you crazy? It was 5:00 in the morning when I asked him to go outside on the balcony. He did and was also blown away by what we saw. First the cross began to disappear even though there was not a cloud in the sky that could block our view. Next, the cross began to reappear only this time a figure of a praying woman also appeared. It was without a doubt Mary at the foot of the cross. What was so miraculous was a number of people were awakened also at that time and saw the exact same thing. Truly, our souls were lifted during this heavenly journey. Here are some special stories.

*   *   *

"Angels for Friends"
-by-
Wally Kulinski

First to put this in context I feel you need to know some facts about me. I am a middle-aged male, married with two sons of which the eldest is married and I am fortunate to have two beautiful grand daughters. I am Catholic and was educated in public schools. I received six of my sacraments (these consist of seven outward signs of God's grace; Baptism, Holy Communion, Reconciliation, Confirmation, Matrimony, Holy Orders, and Anointing of the Sick). To be blunt my spiritual life was more of an obligation until Sue and Jerry Reynolds entered my life.

The introduction to Sue and Jerry actually occurred after waking one morning realizing I needed a birthday present for my business partner and friend, Carolyn. She is very spiritual and Angels have a special place in her heart. I remembered a friend told me about an Angel store near his home in Pennsylvania. I convinced Carolyn to take a ride after work not telling her the destination or reason for this trip.

We arrived at dusk and I didn't even know the store hours but sometimes you follow your gut and go. Well all the buildings in the lot were dark and I said, "Oh boy this is not good."

I was disappointed and then I saw a sign "Calling All Angels" pointing down a narrow driveway. In the distance, there was a building with lights. It was the Angel store but the door was locked.

Normally I would have left to come back later, but deep down inside I knew I needed to knock on the door and hoped I would be able to explain who we were and why we were there. Fortunately, my friend Mike said we could use him as a reference. When a man came to the door, I assuming it was Jerry, introduced myself, apologized for the after hours intrusion, and referenced our mutual friend Mike. Jerry was very gracious and invited us in.

After shopping and being conscious of the time we went to the register and met Sue. After a few minutes of conversation I really felt comfortable talking to her, so I asked her the question . . . why an Angel Store? Sue said, "Angels are special and I can see them with people." Having shared her story with us I asked Sue if she could discern anything about us. She said since you asked she turned to Carolyn and asked if the number "709" had a meaning to her because she sees a man in a field of flowers or perhaps a garden with a big smile on his face and a dog. Carolyn said 709 was the badge number of her brother who was a corrections officer who recently crossed-over after a fatal heart attack. Whenever she sees 709 she feels it represents a message from her brother.

We experienced a great deal in the short time we visited and we expressed our thanks and a desire to return at a later date. It was the beginning of a friendship that has lasted to this day.

Sitting in the car leaving the Angel store Carolyn noticed the time; 7:09 and after arriving home she called me saying that the pick three lottery for the day was 709 which she had played. Some might say an interesting coincidence but we felt it was a GOD-wink and a great deal more.

Our friend Mike had a beautiful wife named Genevieve who was diagnosed with pancreatic cancer and passed away in a relatively short period of time in August 2003. After a few tough months and now with winter upon us, I suggested to Mike that we get together with a few of our friends to spend a weekend at his summer home in Pennsylvania. Hopefully a weekend away with a couple of good meals, drinks, and stories from our past would be a remedy for helping our friend deal with his loss.

The weekend was planned and it began with a Friday night dinner at an English bed and breakfast not far from Mike's home. A light snow had fallen, and there was not a tire track in the snow except ours. The inn seemed deserted with no sign of activity although it was open for business. The meal was excellent for a cold winter night. The aperitifs and cigars near the open fireplace made a great start to our weekend. In fact we said this should have been our Saturday dinner because how can we top this . . . but in fact we did.

Saturday morning, sun shinning and now what to do? We went to breakfast to discuss plans for the day. Joe a banker by profession and friend who came along with us suggested we visit the Angel store he heard so much about. Mike placed a call to Sue to see if she would be at the store. Sue said she did not plan on being there but during her morning prayers it came to her that these four men would be coming to visit her and that they would help her with one of her missions . . . a newly formed food pantry affiliated with the Follow Me Foundation.

We met at the appointed time and after some conversations grabbed some chairs and insisted we follow her. Now the four of us guys were looking at each other saying in expressions, not in words . . . *What's this about?* We only wanted a short stay but down the stairs we followed.

Sue positioned herself in a corner and the four of us were facing her in a semi-circle. After some conversation Sue looked at Joe the banker. I mention his profession because he is ultra conservative and keeps many things to himself.

Sue asked, "What is wrong with the heel of your foot?"

We looked at him as he lurched forward in his chair saying to Sue, "How did you know I'm having a problem with my heel? It is caused by a pinched nerve in my lower back and I'm scheduled to have an operation."

Now we are all friends, but Joe did not walk or show any signs of a problem, and we did not notice a problem. Sue had really gotten our full attention.

Next she focused on Lou who lost his mother some years earlier and said, "Your mother is asking for your understanding and forgiveness because the pain she was experiencing was only countered by her drinking.

Please understand that I love you and I'm sorry." Lou said it was true about his mother that she did have a drinking issue and now it made it easier to understand because his mom never complained about her pain. She just tried to be the best mother that she could be. Now he understood.

Mike had gotten affirmation through Sue that his wife Genevieve was happy in heaven and that he should enjoy his children and live his life.

As for me, Sue felt the presence of Saint Anthony who is my patron saint (typically a saint that we relate well to). I asked many questions about religion, life, and to me it was like having an open confession. My spirit was high, I felt at peace and safe.

Now all this happened when the store was open on a Saturday afternoon and lasted well over an hour—not one customer entered during this time. When we were finished and went upstairs in a very short period of time customers started coming in. Sue said it was not unusual when she was having this type of session.

We convinced Sue and Jerry to join us for dinner that Saturday night. Having a few beverages before dinner I still remember a few questions that we asked Sue, one was, "Why did this occur earlier today? Four guys who have been friends for many years, through you we were exposed to events in our lives that we did not know about each other."

We discussed many subjects during this time together with Sue beyond what was stated earlier in the day. I can say it was a very calm and spiritual experience. Sue repeated that through her morning prayers that she was told by Jesus Christ to meet these four gentlemen and reveal to them her ministry and because we have free will and what each of us does with this knowledge will be an individual decision.

Lou asked does she see good and evil in people. Sue acknowledged that if a situation reveals to her a dark side she tries to avoid it. So yes she can discern good and evil.

Seated at a round corner table with Sue's back to the dining hall a couple walked in behind Sue to be seated at a table next to us. I could see the woman had a nervous condition by uncontrolled shaking of her head and arms. As soon as they passed behind Sue, I could see Sue's face and body becoming animated. When the couple was seated, Sue excused herself and addressed the couple with an introduction that she felt the presence of the Blessed Virgin Mary with this woman who sat before her. Sue asked the couple if she could pray over the woman whose name was Nan and she welcomed the prayer. As Sue prayed, Nan's shaking slowed to a mild tremor. When the prayer was over Sue's face was a scarlet red and she had to excuse herself so as to regain her composure by applying cold water to her face.

The gentleman with Nan was her husband and he had a story for us if we chose to hear it. Of course we wanted to hear it. He proceeded by saying he prayed for a cure for his wife. Early one morning a vision appeared to him in his bedroom. He awoke to see a beautiful woman with jewels covering her chest saying to him, "You need to take your wife to Lourdes or Fatima."

The man said he did not have the means but like a good non-Catholic Englishman he made himself a cup of tea and drew a picture as best he could of what he saw. He took his picture and story to his Pastor and was disappointed with his meeting for he did not receive affirmation to what he had experienced. Nevertheless in a matter of days a business proposal was presented to him that provided the funding for his trip. When he arrived there and saw the Blessed Virgin Mary it became evident that his drawing and vision was of her.

On Sunday, before we concluded our weekend together the four of us sat in Mike's living room reflecting on the events of the past two days. Each of us felt a spiritual presence and it affected each of us with different levels of intensity.

For me knowing Sue and Deacon Jerry has been an epiphany of my spiritual awakening. As a member of The Follow Me Foundation I have learned, giving is the gift. The food pantry has fed the bellies of many as well as nourished their spirit.

I was fortunate to travel with many members of the FMF to Medjugorie to experience where the Blessed Virgin Mary appeared to children in our time. The pilgrimage was a life changing experience.

To know Sue and Deacon Jerry has and will continue to be a privilege that has nurtured my spiritual awaking. They have deeply touched my life.

*   *   *

"Angelic Handiwork"
-by-
Charlie Tahaney

How can I define Sue Reynolds is a person whom God has given a special blessing by being able to speak with Jesus, Mary the Saints and Angels and who would give you the shirt off of her back if you needed it. She has the ability to "see" and hear what has happened and what the future may hold in many people. In our conversations she has told me things about my late dad whom she never met as well as how the spirit of my late father-in-law acted toward my wife, Jo Anne, and I when he passed away.

Sue was there when he died and she saw him put his hand on my shoulder as I gazed at his lifeless body, how he hugged Jo Anne, and how he patted our black Lab Molly on the head as she stood near his bed. I do remember clearly Molly bowing her head as if someone was petting her and at the time I could not understand why. Sue made it perfectly clear the events we had no way of knowing or seeing.

Sue founded and still runs the Follow Me Foundation which spawned the "Food For Friends" food pantry. Unfortunately, due to the economy and not having a permanent site the pantry was forced to close its doors after many years.

Sue's reaction to this set-back was simply, "It's what Jesus wanted for His reasons."

I recall when Sue organized a Sock Hop as a fund-raiser for the Foundation, I was asked to DJ the event. With equipment and cases of oldies, my friend, Bo and I went to help make the evening a success. The theme was the '50's and Sue arrived adorned in a poodle skirt and brown and white saddle shoes carrying a serving tray like the car hops at the old drive-in burger places. It was a memorable evening and it raised a few dollars for the Foundation.

In 2003 we went on a pilgrimage to the town of Medjugorje. One morning we were going to visit Cross Mountain. In order to get there we took a taxi. In Medjugorje the cabs are older model Mercedes-Benz's and wherever you went it was five dollars, around the block or out of town, it was five bucks.

I was sitting in the rear seat, on the right side, Jo Anne was in the middle, and Jerry on the left side. Sue was in the front passenger seat. Upon arriving at our destination I opened the rear door to exit and in order to pull myself up and out, I placed my right had on the center post of the of the four door car. Sue, who was so happy to be there, she exited the car and shut the front door directly on my hand which was still on the post. I saw stars for a moment and figured this was now a crushed hand. I asked Sue to reopen her door to release my hand while Jo Anne went into her RN mode thinking about blood control, stabilization of the hand, reattaching fingers, and the location of the closest trauma center. Jerry's only comment as I recall was "Oh shit!"

I know Sue said a quick prayer and opened the door anticipating the worst as we all did. My hand was released and to everyone's amazement there was not a mark, scratch, or deformation to any part of the hand or the fingers. I gave my hand a quick shake to restore the circulation and upon examination of the vehicle I could see that there was no void or space between the door and the center post. It was steel to steel. It was the prayers of Sue, Jerry, Jo Anne, and myself in addition to the grace of God that this accident did not turn into a severe injury.

Sue apologized over and over again but it was not her fault at all. God was watching me that morning, for which I thanked Him and still do. As for Sue, I told her that I am never again going to ride in a car with her unless I exit first.

* * *

"An Angelic Healing"
-by-
Rose Reese and Betty Ann Flyte

Rose:

In November of 2002, my sister Betty Ann had triple bypass surgery that did not go as hoped. In fact, she had a heart attack after the surgery while in the recovery unit. By March of 2003 all three areas of her heart had re-blocked and she had to have stints inserted. After only three months the stints blocked and she developed congestive heart failure. Her condition was not good and doctors wanted to do a major procedure but they could not continue due to the frailty of her health.

I went to see Sue about the all my sister endured and she suggested we go along on the pilgrimage to Medjugorie. Betty contacted her Cardiologist about making the journey and it was approved! However, she was strongly was advised to listen to her body and avoid climbing mountains.

During the trip, on December 4th after retiring for the day, I woke up to see stars on the wall by Betty Ann's bed, thinking it was a reflection from outside. I realized later that the circle of stars on the wall was shaped just like the ones surrounding Our Lady's head.

On December 5th, as we finished journaling about the day's pilgrimage and turned out the lights, I closed my eyes and felt a pressure on the right side of my far head as though someone was pressing it with their finger. I started to repeat the prayer Angus Dei (Lamb of God) in my head for comfort . . .

Betty Ann:

On this same night as I lay there, a tingling sensation went through my body and exited through my left arm. I did not think much of it at the time but shortly after, it started all over again. At this point I called out to Rose in the next bed.

"Something passed by the bottom of my bed," I said.

Rose looked but did not see anything. I then told her what was happening and asked her to come over to me. She knelt on the floor beside the bed and held my hand between hers.

We started saying the Hail Mary over and over again, and she could feel vibrations going through my body for about half an hour. In feeling the vibrations you could almost tell when they were going to start and stop. When it all subsided, we pushed our beds together. We did not know what to think.

I told Rose not to tell anyone because I was afraid we were getting caught up in the moment of the other miracles taking place while on this pilgrimage to Medjugorie. We fell asleep holding hands.

The next morning we decided to share this experience with Sue. She asked Betty Ann how she was feeling, and assured us we were not imagining things. She had seen six Angels surrounding the bed and the Blessed Mother was there accompanied by the Archangel Raphael, and our deceased mother was looking in from the balcony. Our Lady's hand was over Raphael's guiding him as he massaged Betty Ann's body with his energy.

Once the healing touches started, my mom entered the room. Sue stated Betty Ann was in a progressive healing mode but she should not stop medicines or do anything to over-exert herself. The next day I decided to climb Cross Mountain with assistance and in thanksgiving.

Upon returning home I had an appointment with the doctor. Repeats of the tests were done, and I was told no further procedure was needed on the other stints; in fact, the ejection factor of my heart muscles had improved. This was in 2003 and I am still feeling fine. To this day I have never had any more procedures on stints and no more congestive heart failure.

*   *   *

The Holy Land

Before moving permanently to Wellsboro, PA in 2009, Jerry and I visited our little retreat house every other weekend. On one occasion, we enjoyed the company of our friends Wally and Carolyn and decided to meet some of their Wellsboro friends. This man was a builder who knew many people in the area. I have to laugh as I write that because the town boasted approximately three thousand people. Either way, we met and started to discuss the FMF and our hopes for a retreat house someday.

When we told him about the "Food for Friends" program, he immediately referred me to a woman in Osceola named Sister Jenny.

He also inquired if Jerry was a cabinetmaker as well as a Deacon. Jerry of course said yes and wondered how he knew this. Apparently, at a meeting of some politicians in Harrisburg, the FMF and Jerry were brought up. He was aware that we were seeking a grant to help fund our mission. Small world . . .

On my next weekend visit of rest and relaxation along with my Chihuahua Chiara, something moved me, I call it The Holy Spirit, to gather up my pup and take a ride to Osceola to find this nun Sister Jenny. It was about a half hour drive through beautiful farmland and rolling hills. When I finally got to the town, I found a little grocery store and inquired where I might locate this woman.

"Just down the road about quarter mile, on the left is her shelter, United Christian Ministries," a clerk informed me.

When I got there, it was empty. I knocked loudly, but no one answered. I slowly opened the door and saw a very nice area and hoped there was a restroom available, since I felt as though someone was tap dancing on my bladder from all the coffee I had to drink. Lo and behold, I noticed a restroom and thanked God for small miracles.

After finding a phone number, I decided to head back home and give this nun a call. When I phoned her, she sounded so sweet and agreed to meet. Within two weeks Jerry and I returned to meet this "nun", for lunch. When we arrived, a gentleman with white hair and a mean look on his face greeted us at the door introducing himself as Ed. We told him we had an appointment with Sister Jenny. He kind of looked at us like we were criminals.

Anyway, he proceeded to the end of the hallway and we followed close behind. In the office stood a tiny woman with black-framed glasses and a big smile.

She said, "Welcome, I am sister Jenny and this is my husband Ed." You could have knocked us over with a feather. A married nun? Since when? I of course had to ask how that was possible. She proceeded to explain that in the local community of followers, they referred to her as their sister in Christ and named her, Sister Jenny.

I thought, *OK, I get it now.*

Jenny and I really hit it off from the minute we met. It felt as though we had been friends forever. She and Ed were running three homeless shelters as well as a food pantry. These people were really living out the message of the Gospel. Turns out, Ed was a great big teddy bear of a guy and really had Jenny's back and they became good friends.

Whenever we went to Wellsboro on a weekend, we made it a point to see our new friends. Jenny was also interested in the Catholic faith. She, like many others were told many un-truths regarding the church. As we got to know one another, she began to see that some of those former beliefs were unfounded. She was especially interested in the Eucharist. At one point I had invited them to come to a healing Mass being celebrated by my good friend, Father John Campoli at St. John Bosco's Church in April. They immediately accepted.

Prior to meeting Father John, we had all spoken of a great desire to visit the Holy Land and walk where Jesus and the Apostles had walked. They and fell in love with him and the Mass. At the end of the Mass, a brochure explaining some of the up-and-coming pilgrimages was distributed including one to the Holy Land in September 2008. How awesome it would be to once again be with Father John and Mary for the pilgrimage of a lifetime? Jenny decided she was going, but Jerry and I were financially in a place that was close to bankruptcy.

We knew we could not afford to leave the business, the FMF, and everything else for two weeks, however, we still felt we were being called. It was time to put this matter to serious prayer. Whatever God saw fit to have happen, we would accept, hard as that may be. It is always about trusting in the Lord. On the Fourth of July weekend we got a call from Jenny and Ed about the trip. Jenny told us that she did not want to go without us. We tried to explain our situation but she did not want to hear of it.

She and Ed talked it over and they offered to pay for one of our tickets. Initially, we declined for reasons of pride. Jenny would not hear of it. She wanted to gift us with this and more importantly, she insisted if we did not accept, they were not going. No pressure.

Finally, Jerry and I accepted graciously and thanked our friends for helping to make this dream become a reality.

We boarded the flight to Tel Aviv, Israel and our hearts seemed to be leaping from our chests. For Ed, this was a real treat since he was a small plane pilot and really wanted to experience this flight fully. I took a Valium and out I went. Flying has never been something of a pleasure but more of a necessity for me. Jerry on the other hand began his new role as Kenny Kodak. All I can say, is by the end of the trip, Jerry had taken almost fifteen hundred pictures, this from the guy who hates to take pictures. Go figure.

Unfortunately, due to the nature of my disease, I am like a walking bulls-eye for any and all types of infections, so I had to wear a mask for the entire two weeks which did not help. I still developed a respiratory and sinus infection. However, nothing was going to stop me from enjoying this once in a lifetime experience. As I have mentioned before, the enemy wants to keep us from feeling the presence of God at every turn. It is totally up to us as to how we respond.

To quote Monsignor Esseff, "Tell the devil to go to hell where he belongs."

This was my mindset the entire trip.

While on this pilgrimage we experienced first hand the tensions of the Middle East. Our tour guide in Israel was a Biblical scholar who took us to places most never see. We visited just about every place mentioned throughout the Gospels. We also went to Jordan to visit Petra. This is where we met with some obvious tension against Americans. Our tour guide Omar, made no bones about his dislike—almost hate—of Jews and Americans.

We also had to have an armed guard on the bus we chartered. At one point a young boy was throwing rocks at the bus, as he new we were tourists. The bus stopped and the guard got out and reprimanded the child. It really reminded me how grateful I should be to live in the United States. With all of our political differences and economic issues, it is still the greatest country in the world. Everyday I thank God that I live here.

From sailing on the Sea of Galilee, to Nazareth, to Jerusalem, each step transported us back to over two thousand years ago when Jesus brought this world a Savior; Himself. For me one of the most powerful moments happened when I was able to carry a cross a short way through the Via Dolorosa, the walk to Calvary. It was so overwhelming to imagine how this could have taken place in the exact spot Jesus walked. Each moment carried my spirit to another place.

Never before or since have had I felt such an enormous wave of the Holy Spirit come over me. It was a total gift. If I died at that very moment it would have been OK with me. Nothing else mattered except pleasing God. Now rest assured, surrendering each and every day to The Lord is not easy. Sometimes, I down right fail, but, I keep trying my best always remembering I am not alone on this journey called life.

One of the many miracles of the trip was when we visited the Upper Room where the Holy Spirit came upon the Apostles. There must have been two hundred fifty people from all over the globe speaking in their native tongue in that room. At some point, someone began to sing, "*How Great Thou Art*". Every voice joined as one to praise God. It had not occurred to us until Jenny mentioned at dinner how even though we were of different nationalities, we heard it in English. Perhaps, the others had also heard it in their native tongue? We were unified at that very moment to generations of people who hear the voice of God. What a monumental moment we were blessed with.

All of these accounts are true. All of these miracles happened. All of the relationships formed were because of God and His Divine Mercy. Perhaps this is why the message is continuing through these words. What good is a gift if you never open it and share it with others? As it turned out, Jenny and Ed were so moved by the Masses said in Israel and the Holy experience from the trip, they decided they wanted to explore becoming Catholic. Jerry and I were thrilled for them and eventually were their sponsors. Now Jenny and Ed are happily Ministers of the Eucharist at St. Peter's Church in Wellsboro.

Chapter Eleven

Almost the Final Chapter

It was February of 2010 when The Gentile's offered their home in Florida and plane tickets to us. By this time Jerry and I were living full-time in Wellsboro and he was working at a local home center in the mill shop. I was officially considered disabled and was unable to work outside the home. My illness is such that being in crowded areas or near just about anyone, could cause me to catch the slightest germ and therefore, infection. Most of the time I stayed in the house, save for a trip now and then to the grocery store.

My biggest joy was living directly across the street from St. Peter's Church. At least four times a week I was able to attend daily Mass and spend some quiet time with Jesus. Looking back, this "down" time was exactly what I needed to develop a closer, deeper relationship with Jesus.

Winters were always a very difficult time for me as other diseases and ailments really kicked in. Breathing was becoming very difficult. Of course our financial situation was not making things any easier. One thing was for certain; the entire country was feeling the pinch, so I knew we were not alone. Jerry knew I needed to get into the warmer weather and Janice was right there to offer her place. What a wonderful thing to offer us. Since it was slow at the home center, Jerry and I were able to break away to Florida for a week. We had a wonderful time. I recall sitting on the back porch and basking in the sun when I heard a voice say to me, *"Go to the mountain desert."*

At first I was startled and thought it was a spirit of confusion so I spent time discerning what was said. I prayed deeply and asked Jesus if this was from Him and to help me to understand what this meant. Again, I heard the same words, only this time Jesus clearly told me not to be afraid. Of course this seemed quite strange to me, yet very comforting. I kept this in the back of my mind.

When we returned home, everything went back to the way it was, except, I still had those words, *Go to the mountain desert* on my heart. After checking the answering machine, I told Jerry that his mom called and that he should call her right away. Something did not sound right. Jerry called his mom and she asked if he could meet with her as soon as possible. He and I knew that this was very unusual especially since we lived almost four hours from her condo in New Jersey. After setting up a time to get together, Jerry headed south to Jersey wondering what this was all about. As soon as he arrived, his mom threw herself into his arms hysterically crying. Jerry had no idea what happened.

As they entered the house, she calmed down and went on to explain that while we were away she had an incident with her eyesight and went to the doctor to check it out. The eye doctor did not see anything but suggested she visit with her family doctor. She did and he decided to do some routine tests to be sure everything was OK. She went for a chest x-ray and found out that night she had end stage lung cancer. Naturally, Jerry was as stunned as she was upon hearing the news.

That night when he got home, he and I wept together. Mom wanted to fight this, even though the doctor only gave her six to seven months tops. She fought and fought hard. Everything from radiation to chemotherapy, she wanted to beat this thing. Finally, after six months of this battle, the doctor told her it had metastasized to her brain. There was nothing more they could do but keep her comfortable. By this time Jerry's brother Ed had come from Texas to see Mom and was hoping for a miracle. When Mom decided she did not want any more treatment, we knew she had come to the conclusion that time was short and she just wanted to live out whatever time she had close to her family.

It was not long after the doctor told her she needed full-time care in hospice. She could not wrap her mind around this. She wanted to travel with her friends and enjoy her retirement. She had worked so hard all of her life, how could this be happening? Jerry and I knew she could no longer stay in New Jersey and would need to be closer to us. Thankfully, St. Peter's had a facility called, The Samaritan House, a single home run by volunteers for those who are dying. As it happened, it was available and basically next-door to the church and across the street from us.

It was Labor Day weekend when Mom arrived. At that point she was slurring her words and not always able to articulate. Jerry, Ed, and I were going to be with her as well as the amazing volunteers as she journeyed home.

Mom and I were both born on the same date in the month of November, twenty years apart. We certainly loved each other and got along, but we were never especially close. That was about to change. She and I had a long heart-to-heart and I assured her I would take care of her, especially when she was unable to use the bathroom any longer or bath herself. She was a very private person and there was no way she wanted to have her sons to care for her in that way. I begged God for the strength to do what I would want done for me. He answered my prayer and gave me the strength to care for her in everyway. Truly, I was the one privileged to minister to her. All the time, I knew she was to me, the suffering Jesus.

Jerry and I cried together and leaned on one another for consolation. The hardest part, was knowing that Nan, Jerry's grandmother, would outlive her daughter. Although Mom did not want her mother to see her in hospice, when we went to Stroudsburg to visit Nan, we gathered her things and brought her to see her daughter one final time. None of us could keep from crying watching a 95-year-old woman saying goodbye to her 72-year-old daughter. Michael, Kristina, Anthony and Alyssa had come to say their goodbyes as well. When little Alyssa was only five years old and first heard G-Nan was sick she decided to donate her hair to Locks of Love. Mom could not stop crying when she heard the news. Her little great-granddaughter loved her that much.

Mom's friends called and some came to visit—all would shake their heads in disbelief. Ed needed to go back to New Jersey to prepare for the inevitable. On October 12th we called Ed to say Mom was very close to dying. He left New Jersey and got to The Samaritan

House around 2:00 pm. That morning Jerry and I prayed the Rosary and many other prayers, knowing that was all she really needed from us anymore.

We stood watch as her breathing became very labored. At 4:00 pm, Michael and the family called and we put the phone to her ear. Anthony said, "Have a nice trip G-Nan and don't be afraid". Tears flowed from her eyes. That was the last time she was responsive. By 8:30 pm that evening, Mom passed away. My heart broke for my husband.

It was not long after that we knew Nan, Jerry's grandmother would want to give up. She was living in an assisted living facility in Stroudsburg and basically felt as though she just existed. Of course whenever we went to The Poconos, we visited with her. It was December 2010 when we got a phone call from the facility saying Nan had fallen and they believed, broken her hip.

We are good friends with Dr. Paul Latzko and his wife Louise, who is a nurse and both of them warned that any surgery to a 95-year-old woman would probably not go well. It was two days before Christmas and we were going to be at Michael's for Christmas, so we knew we could visit with Nan that day and find out what she wanted to do. We arrived at the hospital to find her in excruciating pain. She said she just wanted to return to where she was living. Unfortunately, she could not unless she had hip surgery and healed enough where she could return. She had the surgery a few days later and was never the same. She developed sores, infections and the hip was constantly popping out. Jerry was taking a lot of time off to be with her.

We both knew that it was truly by the grace of God that we were able to handle all that was happening. It was only three months after Mom passed that we were facing yet another difficult transition. Nan was sent to a nursing home where she could have physical therapy. It was a disaster. Now I understood why my parents never wanted to go into a nursing home. It was an awful place. After three months, Medicare decided they were no longer paying for her stay, even though she was far from healed. The situation was spiraling downward, very rapidly. It was in May when we moved her to Pleasant Valley Manor where our dear friend Jo Anne Tahaney is an executive nurse manager. Thank God.

Nan felt better knowing Jo Anne was there to help her. Jo Anne immediately accessed her situation and noted all that was wrong with the treatment in the previous nursing home. Jerry and I could at least rest knowing Nan was now in good care. Jo Anne was an Angel.

Jerry and I decided it was time to check out the Southwest—Santa Fe, New Mexico to be exact. We had found a drop dead gorgeous home in Deming, NM on the Internet and wanted to check it out. We had no idea why. Our family was still in Pennsylvania, Nan was in a nursing facility and we were looking at homes clear across the country. We were also wondering what would happen to the FMF. It was then it hit me, Santa Fe was home to the Desert Mountains that Jesus spoke of a while ago. Jerry and I had always loved the Southwest, so perhaps this was where God wanted us. Just in case, I called a friend of mine who was in real estate and asked her to give me an appraisal on our home to let us know what it might be worth should we decide to ever sell.

We happened to be living in the one area of the country that was booming due to the newly found natural gas that was being drilled. After we got the appraisal, we went ahead and made our plans to visit New Mexico in June 2011. Lo and behold, two weeks after we got the appraisal, she had the perfect buyer.

Of course we said, "The house isn't for sale."

She asked if she could bring this woman through anyway, just in case. Sure, why not? Jerry and I felt like we were losing our minds in those days, so what the heck. It turned out the woman loved it. She wanted our house. We did not know what to do except pray. Pray we did and we came to an agreement. If we could not find a house in New Mexico that we wanted, all deals were off.

Just before we left for the airport on June 11th, we stopped to see Nan. She looked awful. She was so sickly looking that we did not know what to think. Jo Anne assured us that if she got any worse she would notify us or Michael immediately.

Before we left, Nan said to me, "Sue, this will be the last time I will see you." I cried all the way to the airport.

When we arrived in Albuquerque, I felt a weird sense this was where I belonged. You should also know we wanted to see these amazing mountains in Santa Fe, based on a song by Paul Simon called "Hearts and Bones"; the mountains are called, Sangre' de Christo or Blood of Christ Mountains.

We met with my cousin Tony who lives in Santa Fe and had a wonderful time visiting all the great sites, especially the Holy ones. Jerry and I were so excited about going to Chimayo, where miracles had taken place. There was a very Holy, special feel to this area that I could not define exactly. It did not matter, when we saw the Sangre's up close and personal, it felt right. Two days after we arrived we looked at some homes in the area. We must have seen twenty with our great realtor, James. He was patient and really wanted to help us.

We had to go to Deming, about four and a half hours south of Santa Fe Before we could make any decisions. We needed a sign. Jerry and I prayed deeply for the right direction. On the way to the elevator in our hotel, Jerry happened to look down and saw a prayer card with a picture of Jesus as the Divine Mercy, with the words, "Jesus I trust in you" written across the bottom. All we needed to do was trust that this was where we were meant to be.

It was not until the day before we were leaving for Deming, James showed us a house that was perfect. The gardens were spectacular and the minute I walked through the front door, I smelled my mother-in-law. She was present and I knew it. I called Jerry aside and told him I thought this was the place because his mom was letting me know. He looked at me like I had twelve heads. I felt this was home, and I wanted to put a bid on the house right away.

We agreed to see the house in Deming first. The next day we packed up and drove four and a half hours to a real estate office in this small town about thirty five miles from the border of Mexico. The wind was whipping and it was beyond hot. I prayed and asked Jesus to let us both know if this was where He wanted us, to let us fall in love with it. Just the opposite happened. The house was situated on ten acres in the middle of nowhere. The wind was blowing dust everywhere at about forty miles per hour. To me this was insane. Thankfully, Jerry felt the same.

We left the agent and went to the hotel. I cried myself to sleep. We were supposed to go straight to Albuquerque the next day to stay overnight for an early flight. Jerry in his wisdom suggested driving an extra hour to Santa Fe to see the two houses that caught our eye, one last time. It was a great idea and James was more than accommodating.

It was a no brainer. We wanted the house with the gardens and lovely interior. We put the bid on it and said our goodbyes. Are we crazy? Yup! We could not wait to get home to tell Michael. Oh, one more thing, we needed to sell Mom's condo in New Jersey if this was to happen. We were on our way to the airport when we got the call we had a buyer for the condo. Without that, we could not have afforded to move. *Thank you God.*

We arrived in Pennsylvania on June 18th with much to try to explain and accomplish. One thing was for sure, we did not want to leave Michael with the responsibility of tending to Nan's needs if we moved—it was something we had to figure out.

On June 22nd, we got a call from Jo Anne that Nan was in the hospital and it looked bleak. Jerry came home from work and he immediately left for the hospital three hours away. Michael went to be with Nan and waited for Jerry. Nan was quickly leaving this earth but something told me she would wait for her grandson, Jerry. He arrived and within ten minutes Nan went to heaven to be with The Lord, her daughter, son, and husband. After the funeral, we quickly began packing for the move of a lifetime. We were going to the mountains in the desert.

At the same time, I received a phone call from the owner of the building of where we were running the food pantry. Mr. Halterman told me he sold the building and we needed to vacate within thirty days. After discussing with the board of directors our options, we realized we had none. We tried repeatedly to secure a permanent location for the food pantry to no avail. Kristina had done an amazing job of running it while we were in Wellsboro but was unable to run it anymore so we made the decision to close. It took every ounce of energy to meet with everyone in Stroudsburg for the last time.

A very large part of me died the day we closed our Food for Friends program. Over ten thousand people a year were no longer able to count on us. I felt as though I failed God and those people. The FMF would continue to help people, even in New Mexico, but this time it would be different.

It was the end of July when the yard sales were done, thanks to the Latzko family. The boxes were packed and we were ready for the movers. Michael, Kristina, and the children came to Wellsboro to say their goodbyes. I thought I would die. I questioned everything we decided, even though I knew this was exactly where the Lord wanted us to go.

How could we leave our family and friends? To make matters worse, our wonderful dog Picolina was thirteen and very sick. The vet told us she would never make it cross-country. We would have to say our goodbyes to my beautiful Pico as well. On August 2nd, we let Pico go to heaven to be with our family. On August 3rd, the movers came and we never looked back. That night we stayed in Williamsport, me, Jerry and Francesca, our Chihuahua. On August 7th we arrived in New Mexico, our new home.

In December, Jerry started an amazing job, or should I say ministry at our new Parish, St. John the Baptist as the Pastoral Outreach Director. I have given an Angel Talk and have started doing spiritual direction again. We continue to seek God's will in all we do. Sometimes we get it right and sometimes we do not. Either way we try to keep Christ first in our lives.

In July 2012 Michael, Kristina, Anthony, and Alyssa came to visit. It was almost a year since we had seen them. They too have moved on, to Pittsburgh, PA to start anew. We still keep in touch with all the people who walked this journey with us. Some have even been to visit. Others promise to visit soon. The FMF contributes to worthy causes in New Mexico and also in Pennsylvania. Jerry and I still seek God's guidance as to where He wants The Heart of Holiness. We have checked out different properties but still wait for His Word. After all, isn't that what really matters most in this world . . . Seek Him first and everything else will fall into place.

This chapter is ending but I pray this book will continue to inspire people to never give up and to always . . . Expect Miracles.

God be with all of you, now and forever.

Chapter Twelve

A Final Word of . . .
Prayers and Angelic Messages!

This book would not be complete unless I shared with all of you the many prayers and messages that were given to me at various times during prayer or just because Jesus wanted me to write down a message. I do not have a timeline on all of them. Perhaps these will provide some insight and comfort to you during your life as they have mine.

*　　*　　*

Eternal Father, Son, Savior of the universe and Holy source of wisdom Spirit. My soul bows before your majesty. My soul honors the creator of life. My soul longs for a deeper relationship and knowledge of my existence in this creation called life. Father, guide my heart, feet, hands, and mouth to your created and perfect will. Jesus, you are all I seek to be. Your essence is the flower of purity. Fill all of my senses with the fragrance of you. Divine Holy Spirit, it is your Wisdom and all of your gifts I truly don't deserve but desperately open my heart and soul to. Holy Spirit cleanse my wickedness and pour out your healing, so when you deem me worthy, those gifts may take root in a clean soul to grow and be shared with others. Amen.

*　　*　　*

No one is totally alone. As long as you can think and feel, you are not alone. I am learning this. Every moment some thought fills my mind and involves others. Sometimes, the thoughts are creative, faithful, and loving. Sometimes, not. Either way, I am never truly alone. I believe the entire created human existence is here with me. Family, friends, and unknowns fill the room. All the ideas can come together if you listen, open up, and allow the visions. I know this sounds crazy. Life is not easily explained or understood. Fancy this, here I am on a beautiful night, a touch from the Sacred and no one to share it with . . . or so I thought.

June 2006

* * *

Almighty Father, creator of the universe, lover of the willing heart, this day August 10, 2006, we humbly submit our entire body, mind, and especially our spirits to your perfect will. Capture us completely to transform us into the beacons of light that you have always intended us to be. Shape us into surrendered subjects of love. Allow your Son to pour healing, cleansing, and refreshing life-giving drops of blood from His Precious hands upon us. Send your Holy Spirit to fill us with every gift from heaven as we prepare to place the armor of God given to us by St. Michael the Archangel upon us to protect us against falling prey to the enemy. May we follow the lead of The Holy Spirit and walk with the entire communion of Saints to forever be changed, and to bring change and love to this hurting world. Jesus, we trust in you. Father, we submit to your creating. Holy Spirit, Holy Trinity, WE ARE YOURS. Amen.

(This prayer was given by Jesus, to me specifically for The Intercessors of the Lamb.)

* * *

Jesus, thank you for being so close to me during this special time we are spending together. My time with you at the Tabernacle today transformed me somehow. What was it you gave me? I felt it slowly entering into my being. Each cell seemed to change. Nothing looks or feels the same. I felt as though I was thread put on a loom and you wove all the threads together. I am changed . . . different. Each thread was intricately woven with the Spirit threads of the apostles, Saints,

147

and all those we hold close to our hearts. I say we, us, our, because my heart and yours are united. In faith, I know this is true. I am holding on to this incredible moment in time. It is no longer living in absence, but presence . . . your Presence. Let's live this life together. I can no longer live a split second without this cardio-attachment. Your sign, the song, "You are My Special Angel". Thank you. Amen.

July 1, 2006

* * *

How can I express my true self to you Lord, when I myself look away from the Truth looking at me in the mirror? If you reside within me, and I truly believe this, why then does fear cripple me when faced with revealing who I am to you and others?

The truth . . . I am a sinner.

The truth . . . I am forgiven by my beautiful Savior.

The truth . . . reconciling this truth, this fact so I may live as a forgiven, loved child of the Creator.

Anything less than this is not recognizing Jesus as true Lord, true Savior, true friend, and companion. For me, it is no longer enough to speak it. No . . . every action of mine must be a deliberate, continuing testimony to this Truth in my life. Is it possible? Yes, because I can accept there will be mistakes. My mistakes that may want to remind me of old sins, old hurts and worst of all, a forgiven past and forgiven life. I may slip on the rocky shores of this life, but I will not stop moving forward into the waters that drown my iniquities and refresh my soul. Amen.

September 1, 2006

* * *

Dearest Jesus,

This day October 23, 2008 we are together again in this beautiful home you have created for Jerry and I and all those who so choose to retreat to the mountains and simplicity of Wellsboro, PA. On our journey here we spoke in depth about the joy of being a very real member of the Most Holy Family. Loving our mother, St. Joseph, and of course you, my Savior. What an incredible conversation we shared. So much joy and no fear. Even as I usually go around the bridge in Mifflinville, I did not because I was with you and my fear was gone.

This beautiful morning I was awakened after a restful night at six. I thought I would be able to go to Mass at 7:30 but you knew that the painter would be here earlier than he said. He was here at 7:30 rather than at 8:00. Again, your gentle guidance kept me where I was needed. I prayed and asked you to please help me with this cleanse of my body and soul. I offered this up for all souls that are in need of cleansing. Only you know the true condition of the soul.

Will I ever be able to thank and praise you enough for all of the many graces you have given to me and my family? You know the deepest crevices of my soul. You continue to be my friend, brother, confident, love, disciplinarian and most of all, my Savior. How can I not thank you daily? Our conversations are always the most interesting. What shall today bring? Mom has made her presence known so strongly. I know she is so loving towards me. Please let her know how much I treasure her offering her motherly love to me. I understand more now than ever.

*   *   *

Jesus said, "Go to the desert." For forty days, what happens? Three temptations. Angels. God will draw near to you. (This was just at the beginning of Lent.) I am taking Jesus with me to the desert. Although I am somewhat reluctant because of the unknown, I am happy for the quiet time. We go with just enough supplies, nothing fancy. Fruit, nuts and water. At first, the time alone with Jesus is welcomed and enlightening. Lots of great conversation. After a short while, He tells me He will be with me in Spirit but will no longer be able to stay in the physical.

Unfortunately, He tells me I will face temptations. I don't want to do this. I hate it.

First temptation: Run away. Milo says, "Stay, He is with you."

Second temptation: Lots of distracting thoughts. Unable to pray as usual. Feeling guilty. Feeling desolate. Don't want to continue.

Saint Michael appears with a sword. The sword has stars around the tip but they are not touching it, they are suspended. He is awesome yet powerful and determined.

He brings the sword close to my heart. This scares me. The stars enter my flesh. No pain. I feel a burst of energy and light flow through me. St. Michael says, "The enemy hates the Light. Stay in the Light and speak, live and prepare for THE TRUTH". He then takes the sword and moves it as though he is doing battle with an unknown spirit. Again I hear, "Stay strong, the third temptation will occur, do not fear, but cover yourself in His Light."

Third temptation: The enemy himself comes. He says, "You are nothing. Give up everything because the vision is nothing, You are stupid and unlovable. He (God) doesn't want you doing the food pantry. That's you wanting this. God doesn't care one bit for you or them. If He did, He would be here. (He points to where he is standing.)

It feels like I can't breathe. It feels like I have no blood running through me. I just want to die.

Then, I hear Milo saying, "Jesus is not standing with the devil because He is standing right beside you."

I answer, "Why can't I feel Him? Why do I still feel so alone?"

He replies, "Because the Truth is not a feeling. It is a knowing. Do you know He loves you? Do you know He is with you, even though you struggle, suffer, and want to run? DO YOU KNOW THE TRUTH?"

"YES, YES, YES! Even in my loneliness I know you are with me. Jesus I do trust in you. I need you. Help me to breathe in life again!"

Immediately, Jesus returns with so many Angels, I cannot count them. They are all smiling and saying, "Faithful soul, rejoice!"

Jesus embraces me. Mom (the Blessed Mother) is now standing next to Him and saying, "My Son, my daughter, my loves."

I have never known such amazing grace and peace. AMEN!

*　　*　　*

I am feeling like I am between worlds. Peter Barone, Mommy, Daddy and Marie (all deceased) and many others are close to me in heart and spirit. Not sure how much time here on Earth, in this body, I have left. I know I must pray. My prayers are full conversations with Mom (Mary) and Jesus. Mom shows me a beautiful place filled with singing, beautiful birds and a magnificent greenhouse.

The sights and smells are breathtaking. Mom asks me to turn around and go towards the corner and look at this one flower. It looks to me like a wonderful sunflower. She says to look deeply into the dark center of the flower. After a few seconds, images of space and the universe begin to emerge.

Stars, galaxies, moons, and things I cannot even describe are everywhere, as far as the eye can see. Mom invites me to take her hand and follow her into the flower. Somehow, we go through and wind-up suspended in time and space. Suddenly, an image of waterfalls, flowers, and a grassy area appear. Within the water I can see icicle shaped crystals with people/souls in them. Is this another glimpse of heaven? Each drop/crystal has someone/something within it.

Then, within an instant, I am back in my kitchen and Jesus is speaking with me. He tells me He is my Savior, sent by the Eternal Father and to trust Him. He knows that I am questioning His voice to be sure it is truly Him and not the enemy. He assures me of His Kingship and dominion over all enemy spirits. I AM Jesus, The Alpha and the Omega. I AM the Savior of the world. DO NOT FEAR. I AM filled with love.

I cry out and beg His mercy and forgiveness. I reveal, once again, my sorrow for having sinned against Him or anyone! He reminds me that He has forgiven the sins I refer to and to come closer to Him. I do, crying, spent, and exhausted, I ask Him to please help Jerry, Michael, Kristina, my grandchildren, and all those who have asked me for prayers. The pain is becoming unbearable.

My concerns for the FMF, the building, my mother-in-law, and all those I pray for. He answers me without hesitation. Trust me, you are being taken care of, as well as those you are praying for.

His final words to me are, "Susan, you are the joy of my heart. I love you."

Jesus, how can I ever thank you. I love you, forever.
June 5, 2010

*   *   *

Fidelity to Spirit

Through sleep The Lord revealed a truth to me:
Fidelity to spirit is deeper than fidelity in the physical form. True love comes from our spirit not from physical/sexual love. That explains the pain felt deep within the soul when we lose a person to physical death. If that love were purely physical, it would not/could not remain after their departure. However, a love that dwells between spirits lasts forever. Faithful to spirit binds for all eternity.

We are loved, spirit to spirit . . . eternal. This is why we continue to seek a deeper connection with one another and to our God. We are challenged to exist within our physical state while growing spiritually; apart from the physical. When we see beauty in nature, animals, etc. we are experiencing an elevation of spirit. We do not own either. We simply are blessed by God through creation. Above all else, seek fidelity to spirit.

We are first and foremost spiritual beings. We live through a physical body in order to experience the human being more fully. This is a temporary state in which a greater lesson is to be achieved. Jesus, is the embodiment of perfection of physical/spirit fidelity.
October 15, 2011

THE *follow me* FOUNDATION, INC.

"Give a man a fish and you feed him for a day, Teach him to fish and you feed him for life."

All proceeds from this book go to the Follow Me Foundation

The **Follow Me Foundation, Inc.** a not-for-profit 501(c)(3) organization, seeks to follow God's command to share our blessings, gifts and talents with the world, as exemplified by Jesus Christ: "Come, you who are blessed by my Father; take your inheritance, the kingdom prepared for you since the creation of the world. For I was hungry and you gave me something to eat, I was thirsty and you gave me something to drink, I was a stranger and you invited me in, I needed clothes and you clothed me, I was sick and you looked after me, I was in prison and you came to visit me." (Matthew 25:34-36)

Using Catholic-based initiatives to serve ALL people regardless of faith or circumstances, the **Follow Me Foundation** offers tangible life-needs such as food and clothing as well as educational and spiritual opportunities to inspire and provide life-affirming values to those who need them most. Ultimately, it is more then just a biblically based philosophy; it is, in every respect, our MISSION.

Donate
We need your help . . . your prayers . . . and your financial support to serve God's children in our community. Please prayerfully consider partnering with The Follow Me Foundation which has a 501c3 tax status. All Donations are tax-deductible.

Donate online
JustGive is a nonprofit organization whose mission is to connect people with the charities and causes they care about and to increase overall giving. Checks and money orders may be made payable to Follow Me Foundation (FMF) and sent to:
Follow Me Foundation
P.O. Box 29774
Santa Fe, NM 87592

Please visit our website www.followmefoundation.org